MEETING PLACE OF THE DEAD

BOOKS BY RICHARD PALMISANO

Ghosts of the Canadian National Exhibition

Ghosts:
An Investigation into a True Canadian Haunting

Journeys into the Unknown:
Mysterious Canadian Encounters with the Paranormal

Overshadows:
An Investigation into a Terrifying Modern Canadian Haunting

MEETING PLACE OF THE DEAD

A True Haunting

RICHARD PALMISANO

Foreword by Peter Roe

DUNDURN
TORONTO

Editor: Carrie Gleason
Design: Courtney Horner
Printer: Webcom
Cover design by Courtney Horner
Cover images © plainpicture/mr. green

Library and Archives Canada Cataloguing in Publication

Palmisano, Richard, author
     Meeting place of the dead : a true haunting / Richard Palmisano.

Issued in print and electronic formats.
ISBN 978-1-4597-2845-5

     1. Haunted houses--Ontario--Halton Hills. 2. Ghosts--Ontario--Halton Hills. 3. Parapsychology--Investigation--Ontario--Halton Hills. I. Title.

BF1472.C3P335 2014   133.1'09713533   C2014-902128-3
                                                         C2014-902129-1

1   2   3   4   5   18   17   16   15   14

We acknowledge the support of the **Canada Council for the Arts** and the **Ontario Arts Council** for our publishing program. We also acknowledge the financial support of the **Government of Canada** through the **Canada Book Fund** and **Livres Canada Books**, and the **Government of Ontario** through the **Ontario Book Publishing Tax Credit** and the **Ontario Media Development Corporation**.

Care has been taken to trace the ownership of copyright material used in this book. The author and the publisher welcome any information enabling them to rectify any references or credits in subsequent editions.

J. Kirk Howard, President

The publisher is not responsible for websites or their content unless they are owned by the publisher.

Printed and bound in Canada.

Visit us at
Dundurn.com
@dundurnpress
Facebook.com/dundurnpress
Pinterest.com/dundurnpress

Dundurn	Gazelle Book Services Limited	Dundurn
3 Church Street, Suite 500	White Cross Mills	2250 Military Road
Toronto, Ontario, Canada	High Town, Lancaster, England	Tonawanda, NY
M5E 1M2	LA1 4XS	U.S.A. 14150

Can You Feel Me?

I can see you but you can't see me.
I am so alone, how can this be?
A soul of the present, a life of the past,
A memory that will never last.

Can you feel me?

I'm here with you as you move on with a smile,
I stand by your side as you walk down the aisle.
A body decaying, I've crossed over the line.
A watchful eye as you live out your prime.

Can you feel me?

I watch as you age, as you grow with a whine,
I watch and I stay but a ripple in time.
A spirit without peace, an Angel in black,
A ruined shirt left to dry on the rack.

Can you feel me?

Life is so precious; you are young, wild and free.
While I am so alone, you've forgotten me.
A soul of the present, a life of the past,
A memory that has failed to last.

Can you feel me?

Hayley Quipp

TABLE OF CONTENTS

ACKNOWLEDGEMENTS

First and foremost, I would like to thank my wife, Michelle, for her continued support of all the crazy things I do and for her help on this and all of my projects — you always keep me pointed in the right direction.

To all the staff at Dundurn Press — thank you for all of your hard work and attention.

To the property owners — thank you so much for allowing us the opportunity to investigate such a mysterious place.

To visiting mediums Carol and Barbara — thanks for coming out and providing your insights into this mystery.

Thank you to Heritage Halton Hills for helping us find the hard-to-locate information.

A big thank you to all the great people in Halton Hills who have assisted and provided information to the team on this project.

To Barbara Ford, who owns the InSpirit Centre, 61 Main St. S. Georgetown, ON, (*www.InSpiritCentre.com*). Thank you for your insights.

To my team, The Searcher Group, who makes going out on these adventures a pleasure. I hope each one of you enjoys this work, as it couldn't have been done without your dedication and tireless contributions. Thank you James McCulloch, Victoria Jamie, Joanna Buonopane, Marilyn Gray, and Dawn Eglitis.

John Mullan — thanks for building some very cool things for the team to use in our research.

Pat Farley — thank you so much for all your help.

To Peter Roe — a big thank you for not only finding this special location, but also for taking the lead in a lot of the work that had to be done; you should feel a great sense of accomplishment.

Thank you to Paul Palmisano, whose dedication to review all our audio/video is an extremely valuable service he provides for The Searcher Group. And thank you for being the class clown, even in the scariest of moments you can always make the team laugh.

To some of the spirits we have encountered and identified at this location — Miriam, John, Nathan, Emma, Dan, Harry, Henry, Amy, and Carol — may you find peace.

For further information on this and other projects as well as to view photos online please go to our website: *www.thesearchergroup.ca.*

FOREWORD

A long time ago, my father shared with me his dual-phrase philosophy on getting ahead in life: "It's who you know" and "It's being in the right place at the right time."

As simplistic as these credos sound, I have to agree, for without either, The Searcher Group would not have experienced the paranormal events you are about to discover.

Halton Hills, Ontario, has a long, varied history with an abundance of stories to be told. I feel blessed to have lived here for most of my life, and after joining Richard Palmisano and The Searcher Group in 2011, I was eager to find work for the team in my own backyard.

The opportunity arrived in the fall of 2012, a week before Richard and I were to meet with Heritage Halton Hills to learn more about haunted locations in the community and to ask for their support while working in the area. I received a series of e-mails referring me to a particular property in a nearby village and to one Google Street View image, in particular.

It was an unassuming house I'd passed a million times, never suspecting it was special, much less haunted. It's not particularly spectacular, picturesque, or even foreboding from the outside. It does have a "warm" feel to it and certainly provokes curiosity from those that choose to drive by more slowly than most. In fact, at our introduction, the homeowners claimed that visitors to the house felt a sense of welcomeness and would often linger, not wanting to leave.

I've often wondered what sort of anomalies the camera cars mapping street views of the world have unintentionally captured. In this case, it appeared that in 2009, while mapping the length of Winston Churchill Boulevard, near Georgetown, Ontario, the Google camera snapped not one, but two ghostly figures on the property we were about to explore. (Unfortunately for the reader, this image is no longer online, nor are the good folks at Google permitting us to publish it.)

The homeowners assured us that no one was living on the property at that time. Suffice it to say, based on this unique find, the team was excited to embark on a new investigation, a new learning experience, and a new chill-inspiring chapter in the company's three-plus decades of existence.

Dad was right, in this case. I hope you enjoy sharing our latest adventure.

Peter Roe, 2014

PREFACE

I have always been fascinated by ghostly activity, and as a small boy growing up in a haunted house I wanted to understand what these whispers and footsteps in the halls when no one was present were. I read everything on ghosts and hauntings I could get my hands on and when I turned eighteen, I founded The Searcher Group — a paranormal research group dedicated to finding these answers. This year will mark our thirty-fifth year of ghost investigations.

How We Do What We Do

I get asked a lot of questions about the work we do in paranormal research and investigations, and one of the biggest questions is why it takes us so long to write our books. The work we do is extremely labour intensive. First we must find a suitable location, one that will interest the reader. Not all locations are haunted and even in some that are, activity may be sporadic or the historical back story just doesn't make for interesting reading. It can take months to find a place that has all the right ingredients for a good story. Once we do find the right location, it takes many more months of investigating, researching, and interviewing to bring you the most complete story possible. We handle these projects like a criminal investigation — verifying information from various sources and making sure we are delivering the facts. This is not always an easy task, as some of our investigations take us deep into history and all witnesses to an event are long dead.

Why We Do What We Do

Why do we investigate the unknown? Academia and mainstream science tell us that ghosts don't exist: we can't see them or bring one into the lab for testing and therefore they can't be real. Sounds simple ... except for the hundreds of thousands of eyewitness reports that have been recorded that suggest ghosts do exist. One has to wonder if something else is going on. Is the topic too sensitive for science to tackle? Or more likely, is a lack of funding for this type of research in the scientific community forcing scientists to deny the existence of spirits? What's interesting is that science has no problem believing that dark energy, dark matter, and, most recently, dark lightening, not only exist but make up the majority of our universe. These are things scientists predict should exist but they have no tangible proof of. So why can't ghosts exist too? To all the skeptics out there that insist ghosts do not exist we say (as my brother Paul nicely summed up), "We don't believe in Skeptics."

I have always liked mysteries and the search for answers, and exploring the mystery of life after death has occupied me for most of my adult life. This has brought me great rewards — making contact with people who have died and remained here to tell their stories, being able to write about what I have discovered, and bringing a small piece of history about someone's past forward to share with you, the reader.

What keeps us going in an investigation is the evidence we gather: events we witness that have no reasonable explanation, recordings of Electronic Voice Phenomena (voices from spirits), and photographs depicting strange phenomena or an apparition. We do this work despite the many hours of work and travel, and the cost. We do it because we feel it is important.

But there is another side to paranormal investigations, the side most don't talk about, and that is the threats and acts of violence from the dead, which may take the form of a sudden onset of sickness or pain (such as the all-too-real sensation of being bitten, kicked, slapped, or scratched) in certain body parts. Though these attacks are, thankfully, short-lived, they can be serious and I have seen seasoned investigators call it quits and never investigate again after a physical attack. I have taken my lumps and continue on my quest to solve these mysteries because people want to know — *I* want to know — what lies ahead for all of us. Oh, and because I can maintain my presence as a royal pain in the backside of mainstream science.

How We Get the Facts

The Searcher Group uses mediums in its investigations. The mediums we use are all independent — with the exception of one pair of mediums that work as a team. Other than that pair, the mediums do not know each other and do not communicate with each other. Information gathered by one medium is recorded in our notes, and at a later date another medium will be used and their data will be compared to that of the first medium. We do this comparison to look for similar data. Even when we have cross-referenced remarkable information from two mediums we still use historical information, witness testimony, and/or Electronic Voice Phenomena (EVP) to further verify what they have said. When all these sources start to come together and form a factual imprint of what may be happening, we start to form the story of a haunting.

EVP, for example, is believed to be sounds and voices of the dead captured on digital or analog tape. (Sounds or voices that are heard by the living in real time are considered "disembodied voices.")

One of the biggest problems we face when we do this work, especially when we use audio surveillance, is that we don't know what we have in the way of EVP until the footage is later analyzed. After it is analyzed, we can use that information to better plan our next visit to the site. *(In this story, EVP recordings are set in italics.)*

Instrumental Transdimensional Communication, or ITC, is an experimental technique using electronic equipment to capture voices or images on video. One method is setting up a camera facing a television and recording a screen that is set to snow or just white noise. If successful, the investigator will capture ghostly voices and images using ITC.

Spirit Box SB-7 is an AM/FM radio that sweeps frequencies extremely fast, between 100 milliseconds to 250 milliseconds per channel. It can also sweep forward and reverse depending on the user's presets. It is believed that if multiple words are recorded over several frequencies then we could possibly be dealing with something paranormal.

Another useful device is a pendulum — a weight suspended from a pivot so it can swing freely. These ancient and very simple items have been used for centuries. The theory behind it is a spirit can use the holder's energy to manipulate the pendulum in either a clockwise or counter clockwise direction. Typically clockwise means a "yes" answer and counter clockwise indicates a "no." A neutral position could indicate no spirit present or one that is unable to provide information to the question asked.

INTRODUCTION

Visions of terrible things creeping around in the shadows, in closets, and under beds can play havoc on your nerves. Things that should now be dead and gone but still linger, just out of sight, bring thoughts of "What do they want?" and "Are they going to get me?" to the forefront of your mind.

Most of our ideas of what ghosts and spirits are is formed in our early, impressionable years by television, movies, and stories told around the kitchen table or camp fire. It's when reality meets imagination that the real terror starts.

However, the majority of things banging about in the middle of the night or, for that matter, even the middle of the day, are at first glance horrifying, but then reason sets in, followed by the realization that most of these ghosts are not so very scary at all.

They are people like you and I, only removed from their physical body. They may be deceased relatives or strangers whose old home we have just moved into and now call our own. Many of these ghosts have a story to tell; some are trying to voice an opinion on what you may be doing in or to their last place of residency; and others just want us to acknowledge that they exist. But for whatever reason ghosts exist, it is fascinating and life changing to discover that life continues well beyond our physical tenor in this plane of existence. But until we break down our old, preconceived ideas of what ghosts are, our encounters with them will always cause fear.

I would like to tell you that the story you are about to read is not scary at all, but that would be untrue, just like I would like to say that there are not bad things, evil things, lurking out there … because there are.

1

PRE-INVESTIGATION
EARLY FALL

Peter called; he had a lead on a property that appeared to be haunted. The chain of information began with an image captured by the Google Street View car that drives the endless grid of streets to map their service of Street View addresses. It seemed that while mapping a street about thirty-five miles west of Toronto, Ontario, in a farming community on the border of Georgetown, they had photographed two ghostly specters on a property. This information found its way to the building's owners, who confirmed that the building was not in use and was unoccupied at the time. The images showed a man through the living room window and an older female in early twentieth-century period clothing standing at the front door.

Peter had secured access to the property and building and had arranged for our first visit. He also informed me that the owners had removed a two-storey wooden shed from the property, and that they had discovered an old pistol hidden in a wall that would be at the property for us to examine.

The cottage on the property was on the brink of being designated as an historical building. When that happened, there would be renewed interest in it from the public. We had to act fast to conclude our investigation into the paranormal activities there, while it was still "quiet."

2

FIRST INVESTIGATION
NOVEMBER

Paul, Marilyn, and I arrived ahead of the rest of the team, so we took the opportunity to have a look around the property while we waited for them. It was still light out but was quite cold with a slight wind coming from the northwest. The main structure was a cottage built in 1840, as a Scottish Baptist church. We circled the building, paying attention to the windows and doors and looking for any activity within. We found none.

The building had a stone rubble foundation, the exterior walls a greyish-beige stucco covering the original round log construction. The design appeared to be salt box with clear modifications done over its long history. The front porch, probably added in the 1920s, had a cement floor pad and craftsman-style, square-tapered columns on top of stone piers. We stood in the street and compared the front of the building to the photo taken by Google Street View and could clearly see where the alleged spirits appeared to be standing at the instant the photo was snapped.

Out back was an ancient barn, although not as old as the cottage. We decided not to enter the barn, but remained outside until the rest of the team arrived.

I found an old well not far from the house, which was capped off and now sported several dying potted plants.

Soon after, Victoria and Peter arrived on-site. Peter had the key and we entered the cottage by the back door, into the kitchen. It was obvious that the cottage had under gone numerous renovations and upgrades over the years. The back part of the cottage, where the kitchen was, had been added around 1890. Peter explained that the building had been moved to its current location in 1873 from about two miles away. The team did a quick tour: on the main floor was a powder room; a kitchen that opened up onto the main room, or studio as it was currently called; and two mid-sized rooms on the north side. Stairs led from the main room to the second floor and we filed up them. At the top of the stairs was a large open area, to the right was a small bedroom, and at the rear of the building was a larger bedroom with an ensuite bathroom. The floor was uneven underfoot.

The team fanned out to different rooms in the cottage and prepared their personal equipment — digital cameras, digital recorders, and gauss meters for reading electromagnetic fields. Paul wanted our first camera set up in the rear bedroom, facing toward the large open area and the stairs. The high-quality, built-in microphone on this camera would capture all sounds of movement and, hopefully, Electronic Voice Phenomena (EVP). Paul checked the lighting and gave me the thumbs-up sign to begin recording. Next, Paul and I moved downstairs to the front entrance and set up a second camera facing through the main room toward the stairs. The built-in microphone on this camera was designed to pick up sounds as low as 15 Hz, with this frequency we would be able to record sounds and voices outside of our normal range of hearing. (Human hearing is from 20 Hz to 20 KHz.) We placed a third camera in the kitchen facing the back door. Our audio/video surveillance was now live and recording.

As we were setting up, Peter told us some of the history of the building and the move from its original location to where it now sits. In its long history, the building had been used as a church, a private residence and farm, a rental home, and a business. Peter had pulled a list of names of people associated with cottage from the local archive, but it was incomplete. As Peter started to describe how the cottage had been moved, Paul, standing near the base of the stairs, heard a male voice from upstairs say, "Yes."

Paul moved quickly up the stairs and looked past the large open area to the camera. Nothing was there. None of us were on the second floor at the time we heard the voice, and since we had searched the second floor just moments ago, we knew there no human intruders in the building. Was it the voice of a spirit agreeing to what Peter was saying about the building's history?

Victoria entered the northwest room on the main floor and immediately felt nervous. She wasn't frightened; just a nervous feeling washed over her. As she stepped out from the room the feeling vanished.

Joanna, one the team's mediums, arrived on-site.

[As Peter welcomes her into the kitchen, his digital voice recorder is hit by a charge of static.]

Joanna handed Peter the Google Street View photo that he had sent to her earlier. As a medium, Joanna is sensitive to spirit energy and can receive psychic impressions from photographs.

"So, what did you get [from the photo]?" Peter asked.

"Interesting," she replied. "I felt an older European couple and the husband was very abusive; a strong man, not fearful. This house was his, the wife was his property — that kind of mentality. He's not scared of us and his presence is all over the place."

[Male voice EVP: "Right."]

[As Peter and Joanna talk in the kitchen, a male voice is captured on audio saying "Plain Friday."]

When this EVP was later reviewed, we were unsure who he was talking to or what the meaning of this phrase was. Was it meant for us?

Paul, Victoria, and I moved to the bottom of the stairs and were about to enter the kitchen when all three of us heard a woman briefly humming, but unfortunately this was not captured on any of our recording equipment. Because it was not captured in a recording, this was not an EVP. Instead, it is considered a "disembodied voice" because it was actually heard by us in real time.

I looked to Paul, who raised his eyebrows, and I knew he was thinking the same thing I was: two physical manifestations of voice in such a short time. This place seemed extremely active. There was no telling at that time what we might encounter next or what EVPs were being captured.

Peter and Joanna moved toward the studio. Peter said, "So this male ..."

"He's just following us, so where we are, he's going to be," Joanna stated.

[There is a static burst on Peter's digital voice recorder.]

Joanna looked back toward the kitchen and said, "Not so much in the kitchen, that wasn't his place."

Joanna stepped into the studio. "He tolerates the people here. He is curious and has some intrigue about them. If he wanted them out, they'd be out."

Peter stopped and looked around.

"What's the matter?" I asked him.

"I felt like I walked into a cobweb. It touched my forehead."

Everyone had passed through this doorway many times since we arrived. We examined the doorway, the ceiling, and Peter's hair, but found no evidence of a spider web. It had been observed at other haunted locations that a spirit's energy may cause a person who comes into contact with it to feel as though they had walked into a spider web.

Walking into the northwest room, where Victoria had felt the "nervous feeling," Joanna was quick to report experiencing a shiver. "I am getting constant shivers here. I think he spends a lot of his time in this room." Joanna leaned against the west wall, facing the front window. "I think he would watch out the window so that he could see out, but not be seen. He thinks people can still see him. I think he did this with his wife as well, to monitor her. I am not getting a name though."

Marilyn moved to the northwest room and stood in the doorway. She gasped involuntarily, but said nothing.

Joanna looked at Marilyn and exhaled loudly. "I think it's just his energy all around us."

"Oppressive?" Peter asked.

"Not necessarily. I am surprised. I assumed it would have been, yet it's not. I almost feel like he lost his aggression when he lost his wife. Or maybe just because so much time has passed. He just couldn't control anybody now. But he still likes to think that he is in control, so that is why I said if he wanted the people here out, they would definitely be gone."

"Do you think he likes our company?" Peter asked.

"No, no. He's curious only, but he doesn't like what I am saying. It is, quite frankly, pissing him off," Joanna said.

"Is he speaking to you?"

"I'm feeling like he is, um … a little more combative because he could only beat up his wife.… Not so strong anymore … Oh, he didn't like that."

Peter moved past the northwest room as Marilyn stepped out and reported that she felt it was claustrophobic.

[The voice of a male is recorded on Peter's digital recorder: "They had me."]

"I don't fear him though, because I don't think it's anything we can't handle," Joanna stated.

[Three quick bursts of static are captured on Peter's digital voice recorder.]

"He was able to antagonize and abuse his wife, but that doesn't mean he's capable of doing that to [just] anyone — you know what I mean? They [the spirits] think they're strong in their own mind." *[Another burst of static.]* "Really they are cowards!"

"That is awful," Marilyn interjected.

"The wife was so abused," Joanna stated.

[The digital recorder captures a gravely sounding male voice grunting and saying: "Aw."]

[Victoria's digital recorder captures the sound of a clock ticking eight times, though there is no clock in the house.]

"She was a frail thing," Joanna said, looking around.

"No name yet?" Peter asked.

"Well, it's like Elizabetha, or something like that popped into my head. European ... Eastern European," Joanna stated.

"Right. Ukrainian?" Marilyn asked.

"Something like that."

Victoria reported from the northwest room that she felt pressure in her head.

Marilyn caught something moving out of the corner of her eye, like a flash of light passing over our heads.

[Whispering is caught on Victoria's recorder and then two more ticking sounds.]

Paul was standing in the living room and reported feeling tingling on his left side. I scanned the area with my gauss meter and detected a reading of .3 to .4 milligauss. The reading came and went however close to the ceiling. I detected a reading of 1.1 milligauss, which was attributed to a hidden electrical line. However, when Paul moved away from the area the readings went to zero, except at the ceiling.

[Peter's digital recorder captures the sound of a woman moaning.]

The team headed upstairs.

[A male voice says something unintelligible that is recorded on the main-floor surveillance camera as we climb the stairs.]

Most of the team moved into the large rear bedroom, trying to stay out of the way of the surveillance camera. Marilyn stopped at the top of the stairs and hung back in the large open area with Joanna.

"Hmm. Okay, this is his secondary area where he spends time. This used to be the master bedroom," Joanna said, looking around. "I feel they were here for quite a few years on this property. That is why he claims ownership over it. He might have built this place. It's his land, you know, and land is important."

Peter moved closer to Joanna. "By length of time what do you mean?"

"Until the day he died."

"But how long ago? When you say for quite a long time, a hundred years, or …?"

"Perhaps sixty…. Oh, no, no."

"Within a hundred years?"

"Yeah, no. Umm…." She paused. "See I'm not getting … I got her in the '40s, I didn't get her before that, even though the property might have been around, he came in. I feel like, in the 1940s and stayed until about the '60s or '70s. So I don't know. He claims the property as his, though. Even though the house might have been here for a hundred years, unless he did enough renovations to it and enough changes to the property, he feels that it was nothing before him. You know what I mean?" Joanna said. "I also feel he is a very unsettled personality; he could never rest, always uptight, concerned about every little stupid thing that he couldn't control." Joanna looked out the window. "I doubt that he was very social with his neighbours. It is hot in this room."

Marilyn moved into the master bedroom and walked toward the bathroom. Peter joined her.

[There is a long breathy whisper on Victoria's recorder.]

Peter and Marilyn entered the bathroom.

[Male voice EVP: "Get out."]

I set up the Spirit Box, which is a device designed to scan through radio signals at a 100-millisecond sweep. This particular time the unit was set to FM frequencies with a reverse sweep. The idea is that as the unit sweeps through these frequencies at such a fast rate, it produces white noise that allows us to capture spirit energy communicating.

Paul started working on setting the lights on the upper floor to optimize the camera view. "That will cut any glare."

Peter suggested some lighting options. [His digital recorder captures a female voice saying quickly, "That's a spike."]

Joanna walked into the bathroom and pulled the shower curtain open. Inspecting the tub, she said, "He would violently rape his own wife."

"In this area?" Peter asked, moving in beside her.

"Yeah."

"Is that right?" Peter yelled out.

[A "yep" comes immediately over the Spirit Box.]

There was a bang from downstairs, and everyone looked at each other.

"Is that the furnace coming on?" Peter asked.

"Can't be, something is moving downstairs," I replied, moving to the doorway to get a better position from which to listen.

"I thought I was hearing something through the vent, like something starting up," Peter said.

"No, it's something moving down there," I whispered.

"That's good, let it move," Paul said.

On the main floor, surveillance camera activity was being recorded.

[There is a clicking sound, then a male says, "Miriam" — pause — "They are all alive." The voice fades away and the rest of the message is lost.

An older female voice replies, "Ooooh" — pause — "Thank you."

The camera captures the creaking of the main floor.

Male voice: "Where are they?"

Female voice: "Upstairs."]

We noticed flashes of light on the upstairs camera and small orbs flying about the room. The light flashes could have indicated something passing the camera; however, the orbs were nothing more than dust particles reflecting the Infrared illuminators (IR) back into the lens.

I asked Marilyn to shut off the main upstairs light. She walked over and toggled the switch off.

On the main floor, camera activity was being recorded.

[Immediately, a male says, "Stay there" — pause — "Are you okay?"

There is no reply. However, there are footfalls near the main-floor camera.]

We headed back down to the main floor.

"Us being here will start something," Victoria stated.

"Upset him ..." Joanna said.

We all moved into the kitchen. Peter pulled a drawer open and took out a small hand gun. He handed it to Paul, who examined it.

The pistol was extremely rusted, the grips rotted away. Paul passed it to me and I checked to make sure there was no ammunition in the cylinder. It was empty.

Joanna took the gun and held it in her hands. "I sense … him. Not anything off this [the hand gun]. He is around, laughing. He is saying, 'Oh, I wish I would have used it.' He used this as a threat; never used it against anyone. 'I wish I would have. I was gonna, but didn't.' That's what I am getting from this. He used it as a threat, didn't actually use it or killed anyone with it. It was just for him to feel like a big man.

"I think this was here before him even, and he found it. That's all I am getting. I am tuned into him right now."

"I can't see having a gun in here when this building was used as a church," Paul said.

"Does anybody belong to this gun?" Paul asked aloud. "Do you know anything about this gun?"

There was no reply.

"This looks like it's over a hundred years old," Joanna said.

"That's what I'm thinking," Paul said.

"Have you seen this gun before today?" Paul asked aloud.

"Did you do all the renovation work to this place?" Joanna asked.

No reply.

Peter set up an E. Probe in the living room under the watchful eye of the surveillance camera. (The E. Probe device is used to detect electrical energy in either very close proximity or by touch, depending on the sensitivity setting.) Then he placed his digital voice recorder on the table.

The team prepared to leave the house. Everyone filed out the back door and Peter, being the last one to leave, called out, "We are going." Then he pulled the door closed.

We headed out, past a massive gnarled tree, to the ancient barn. Peter pulled the door open and chained it, and we all stepped inside. The main floor was divided into several areas. There were stairs to a root cellar and a fixed ladder leading to a large loft above. The team fanned out, taking photos while exploring the barn.

It was interesting to note that we captured the meowing of a cat, and although we were in a country setting in an old barn, where one would expect to hear a cat, no living cat was seen. However, Peter discovered the mummified remains of a cat in the cellar.

At that point, the team headed off to tour another location that was brought to our attention as possibly being haunted. Peter had arranged an introductory tour that would take us away from this location for about an hour. We were confident that our equipment left operating in the cottage would capture any activity in our short absence.

Meanwhile back in the cottage …

[From the surveillance camera microphone, the floor starts to creak in the living room as if someone is walking and shifting their weight. Then the E. Probe activates several times. The camera captures the little red indicator light come on and the alarm sound, but no other activity.

Peter's digital recorder picks up movement and a scratching sound, a light tap near the recorder, then a strange sound as if someone's stomach is growling.

After a few minutes more, there is movement near the recorder, and sounds as though someone is going through Peter's equipment case.]

During our absence from the building, there was an enormous amount of unexplainable sounds recorded within the house: banging, walking, the sound of fabric rustling, someone coughing and sneezing, and a very distinct sound of someone taking off either boots or heavy shoes and dropping them to the floor one at a time.

The team returned and entered the house.

Peter, Joanna, Victoria, and Marilyn headed upstairs. Paul and I remained on the main floor and checked the cameras.

Paul discovered none of his LED flashlights were working, and when we changed the batteries they still would not work. I loaded the same batteries into my flashlight and they worked fine.

"But they were just working before we left," Paul stated.

[Peter's digital camera is still recording in the living room and captures two knocking sounds and something shifting near the recorder. The E. Probe activates, but the alarm is muted and neither Paul nor I notice the flashing red light on the device.]

Peter came down and saw the E. Probe light and told us of the alarm activation.

"I've never seen flashlights go like that before," Paul said, a little upset.

"I know," I agreed.

[*Peter's digital camera records a loud male voice, either clearing his throat or saying "uh-huh."*]

Peter and Paul entered the northwest room. Paul called out, "Hello?" No response.

"Do you want us to leave?" Paul asked aloud.

[*A desperate-sounding female voice says, "Yes."*]

"Is there someone here with the surname Smith?" Peter asked.

There appeared that a female responded "Yes," but due to the sound of the refrigerator motor starting at that exact same moment it was unclear.

Peter asked, "Do you want us to leave?"

[*EVP response: "Hell ya!"*]

We moved through the house and everyone ended up on the second floor.

"The place seems so quiet," Peter stated as we all sat around in the upper floor bedroom.

[*The recorder captures the sound of someone walking on hardwood, even though the floors are covered in wall-to-wall carpet on this level. A total of six footfalls are recorded.*]

The sound of a female moaning was heard by everyone in the room. Unnerved, the team moved out to check the floor. Nothing was found.

There were loud knocks coming from the main floor, which were heard by Peter, Joanna, and Marilyn. Paul moved to the top of the stairs and confirmed he heard someone walking down on the first floor.

Joanna moved to the top of the stairs. "Who's with you?" she asked. No reply came.

[*As the team starts to move back downstairs to the main floor, the main-floor camera captures a male voice saying, "Win."*] Upon later analysis of this EVP we were at a loss as to what this may have meant. It would seem that a lot of what we recorded was not for our benefit, but rather communication between the spirits themselves.

Paul walked over to the wall switch and turned on the large overhead light. This must have upset something within the house.

[*It is followed by an immediate EVP on the main-floor camera of a male voice saying, "Damn it, I'll get you."*]

Peter and Paul moved farther into the living room and spoke to one another.

[*The digital recorder captures unknown talking over their voices, the content impossible to understand.*]

Paul looked over at me. "I just heard a voice."

"What did it say?"

"I don't know."

On review it seemed that it was an agreement with what Peter was saying. It was simply a voice of an unknown male saying, "Yeah."

"We should head out to the barn and do some work out there," I told the team.

[As we prepare to head out, the surveillance system captures a male voice saying, "Yeah, Miriam," and the sound of walking.] The camera footage clearly showed the team standing near the kitchen entrance, none of us were moving.

We headed out into the frigid night air and made the short trek to the barn. I pulled the door open and latched the chain to an old, rusted piece of metal nailed to the side of the barn. The team entered, split up, and investigated the barn.

Paul immediately headed up to the loft to investigate and take photos. He also wanted to make sure that it was safe for the rest of the team.

From the doorway, Marilyn captured a photo of what seems to be a person near the loft ladder. Looking at the image on the camera view finder, it seemed quite convincing, however upon later review of this photo on the computer system it turned out to be nothing.

Several of us moved down into the cellar for a quick look.

[Peter captures a whisper on his digital recorder. Standing quietly in the stable area, he also records a shuffling sound and a male saying, "Break it up here," or "Bring it up here." Then wood creaking as something in the room moves.]

We didn't know about the EVPs captured in the barn yet, so we felt that it was very quiet and, factoring in the cold, we headed back to the house.

We all re-entered the cottage.

I wanted to attempt communication using the Spirit Box again, so we set up in the small room on the north side of the main floor.

I set the box to scan all FM frequencies for 100 millisecond per channel.

Peter jumped right in and started asking questions: "Is Isabella is here?"

Spirit Box: There was a "yes" in reply.

Peter called out, "Is Isabella here? Can I speak with Isabella?"

Spirit Box — a female voice, breathily: "Yes."

"Isabella?"

Spirit Box: "Yes."

"May I ask you about the gun?"

Spirit Box — faintly: "Yes."

"You're not afraid of the gun, are you?" Peter continued.

Spirit Box: No response.

"Does the gun belong to an owner of this house that came after you?"

Spirit Box: "Yes."

"Did it belong to a 'Smith'?"

Spirit Box: "Yes."

"What was his first name?"

Spirit Box: "Luke."

[Peter records a husky-sounding male chuckle.]

"Isabella, are you still with us?" Peter asked.

Spirit Box: No reply.

Spirit Box — a male voice: "We're alone."

Paul was by the door to the main room, looking out. He said, "I just saw a shadow on the stairs!"

We all, except Peter, rushed to investigate.

I had shut off the Spirit Box but was still carrying it. I led the team up the stairs, and as I came to the mid-landing, the Spirit Box screamed to life, startling us all. I shut it off again and we proceeded up.

It was interesting to later watch the events unfold from the surveillance camera footage: the main-floor camera captures a shadow moving up the stairs very quickly, Paul calls out he sees the shadow on the stairs, and we all follow it.

[The second-floor camera at that same moment is enveloped ever-so-briefly by a blackness, as if something is blocking its lens.]

Then we arrived on the floor.

After we searched the upper floor and found nothing, there was a flash on the camera, then an older male talking. We could not make out what he said.

[A female clears her throat but says nothing.]

There were several more flashes and then Joanna saw two orbs move across the screen. These were not dust, as they were large and yellow in color.

Paul called out, "What's your name?"

[EVP on surveillance camera: "Bill."]

"I feel something," Paul stated.

Peter continued asking questions on the main floor, now using his own Spirit Box.

"Should I go up there?" Peter asked.

Spirit Box — a male voice: "Uh-uh."

"Isabella, are you still here with me?" Peter asked.

Spirit Box: A slight sound possibly indicated a "yes."

"Is Willie buried at the Hillcrest cemetery?" Peter asked.

Spirit Box: No reply.

We all returned to the main-floor studio.

[The upstairs camera records walking on the upper floor.]

There was an audible bang. Peter stopped and looked around. "Did you hear that?"

"Yeah," Paul said.

"None of us were moving," I reported from my position at the door to the room.

"What is your first name?" I asked.

[Male voice: "First name."

Pause.

A male voice saying, "Leave us, leave us," is recorded on the audio surveillance.]

"What can you tell us about this Smith person?"

["Bad," says an EVP of a female voice. It is followed directly by a male EVP saying, "Good."]

After the events, we felt it was time for a break to regroup and collect our thoughts. We left the equipment operating while the team headed out to get some food.

The house went quiet.

But when we returned could hear from outside the E. Probe alarm sounding.

Peter entered first to check his equipment; all seemed to be in order.

The house had grown quiet and the team started to pack up.

[Peter's digital recorder captures one last EVP, that of a woman: "Leave mah home."]

Conclusions:

Although I was convinced that this location was extremely active, it wasn't until several days after our investigation when I started to receive analysis reports from the team that I was sure. Here's what we concluded from our first investigation.

- After reviewing the data collected from the surveillance cameras, digital voice recorders and Spirit Box session, it became abundantly clear that we were onto a major haunted location — there seemed to be many spirits there.
- Not only had we recorded many high-quality EVPs — including a male voice in an astonishing EVP saying, "Miriam, they are all alive" — we also captured footage of a "shadow person" that had moved from the living room to the second floor.
- Most of the team experienced disembodied voices.

I did a quick comparison of haunts I had been involved in over the last thirty-five years. It had been more than ten years since I had seen this level of activity on a first visit — not since the investigations reported in my first book, *Overshadows*. The prospect was incalculable. This was only the beginning, however, and none of us could imagine what lay ahead.

3

SECOND INVESTIGATION
DECEMBER

Peter, Paul, and I arrived early and met with the property owner to go over some of the early history of the house and the property.

As we stood in the kitchen talking, I looked out the back window and could see that a storm was brewing: the wind was now carrying leaves, dirt, and debris, and the sky was charcoal. I noticed right away that inside the house was virtually silent, probably attributed to the heavy construction of the old place with its eighteen-inch-thick walls. Paul showed the owner a few photos that we had taken in the barn on our last visit.

[Peter's digital voice recorder captures a gruff male voice saying, "Me, have a see."]

The owner departed, wishing us luck in our search. The three of us went out to the vehicle to bring in the equipment; Peter laid his digital recorder down in a small alcove at the base of the stairs. *[As we exit, the recorder captures a click and subtle movements.]* We set up our surveillance equipment as we had during our previous visit and went outside to wait for the rest of the team to arrive.

Victoria and her twin sister, Stephanie, who was joining us for the night, arrived and we all entered the house together.

The team split up and Peter set up his E. Probes as Victoria took her sister upstairs for a tour of the house. Paul and I took random photos.

The girls came back down to the main floor. "I got a different feeling up there this time. A very comforting feeling, but that little room at the top of the stairs, which was fine last time, was very uncomfortable," Victoria reported.

"Which room did you go into first?" Peter asked.

"The big one at the back, where the camera is."

Paul started to lay talcum powder in strategic locations around the house. He placed a large black garbage bag down on the floor and generously shook out the powder to cover the bag in the hopes that we would get an imprint of a footprint in the powder.

Peter's E. Probe went off, and as he reset it he explained how it worked to Victoria and Stephanie.

[Peter's digital recorder captures a female sighing.]

We decided to go outside and tour the exterior of the house and examine the front porch. Peter placed his digital recorder on a chair in the northeast room near the window and we all headed outside.

[After a few minutes of silence there are sounds of movement caught on the recorder and then the persistent squeaking like that of small wheels.

The sounds of movement are very close to the camera — rustling sounds — then a male voice calling, "Jimmy."]

The E. Probe went off and Peter went back in to check it.

As we were standing outside, Paul saw a black shadow pass the upper window facing the driveway. I immediately thought it might be Peter, but at that exact moment Peter pulled the back door closed. Paul suggested that the camera set up on the second floor may have captured something. After watching the second-floor windows for a few more minutes and seeing nothing further, we all headed off to the barn.

[Inside the cottage there are still sounds being recorded by the main-floor camera.

Rustling of material.

Male EVP: "Miriam."

No reply.]

The team entered the barn and spread out, taking photos and using their digital recorders in an attempt to capture any activity.

Victoria headed down into the root cellar of the barn. She heard walking and as she glanced up, she saw two legs passing the open door heading deeper into the interior of the barn. She immediately came up and found the rest of the team in the loft taking photos.

"I just saw someone walk past the cellar door on the main floor," she called up to the rest of us.

Paul looked down through the open hatch at her, "There was no one down there."

I climbed down and joined her. We walked the main floor and found nothing.

As we descended the stairs into the depths of the barn we noticed the mummified remains of the cat Peter had mentioned. A bare bulb hung from the centre of the ceiling. There was a well-defined hump in the dirt floor three feet wide and approximately six feet long.

"So who's buried here?" Paul asked, standing on the hump.

Everyone was thinking the same thing about this mound it seemed, but Paul was the only one who said it out loud. "So, when do we dig?"

"We would need permission first," I replied.

"We could talk with the owners," Peter said.

I nodded my head yes and the team moved up the stairs to the main floor of the barn.

The team left the barn and we were now standing around in the driveway next to the house. *[Inside there is the sound of a heavy object being dropped to the floor and Peter's E. Probe goes off.]*

[The camera captures the sound of loud knocking, the snapping of fingers, tapping, and movement on the floor. Then a male's voice calls, "Henry."]

Peter led the way back into the house as he wanted to check the E. Probe on the main floor. The rest of the team headed upstairs.

[Indecipherable talking is recorded by the camera's microphone and then a male's voice saying, "Ya."]

Peter started up the stairs.

[A heavy breath next to him, like an exhale, is captured on his digital voice recorder.]

[Directly behind the camera on the main floor, the door handle turns several times. It sounds like the door opens, although there isn't enough room as the camera is positioned there. Then the sound of movement behind the camera.

Male EVP: "They're all alive."]

The team settled into the large master bedroom on the second floor. Besides the camera and two folding chairs, there was nothing else in the room. Some of the team sat on the floor as we prepared to conduct a Spirit Box session.

After ten minutes of Spirit Box session without any noticeable results, the team took a break on the main floor.

Peter checked his equipment in the kitchen. *[His digital recorder captures the sound of the catch on the equipment box clicking, banging against the side of the case; no one was near the case at the time.]*

The team re-assembled in the northwest room on the main floor for a second try at a Spirit Box session.

I set the box for 100-millisecond sweep FM channels in reverse. As the team waited and listened, there was a faint "Hello" heard over the speaker.

There was a pause.

Me: "Did that say, 'Hello'?"

Victoria: "That's what it sounded like, yeah."

Me: "Yeah."

Spirit Box: "Yeah!"

Me: "Hello?"

Spirit Box: "Hello."

Peter: "Was that 'Hello' again?"

Me: "How are you?"

Spirit Box — a female voice, pleasant-sounding: "Fine."

Sprit Box — a gruff male voice: "Go to Hell!"

Peter: "Pardon?"

Me: "How are you today?"

Spirit Box: "Well."

Me: "My name's Richard. What's your name?"

Spirit Box — a male voice, immediately: "Chris."

Spirit Box: "We heard them."

Spirit Box — a young male, possibly with a Scottish accent: "That's enough!"

Spirit Box— young female: "Jesus!"

Spirit Box: "Alena!"

Peter: "What is your name?"

Spirit Box — young female, immediately: "David!"

Spirit Box — a gruff male voice: "Alena!"

Spirit Box: A loud burst of static that sounds like china breaking. Then a woman's shriek.

Spirit Box: "Go!"

Me: "Do you mind that we're visiting today?"

A twelve-second pause.

[The camera captures a male voice saying, "Get out."]

Victoria: "Is it okay that we're here?"

There was a long pause.

Spirit Box — a young male, timid-sounding: "Yup."

Spirit Box — a female voice: "Honey!"

Spirit Box — a male, deep voice: "Yeah."

Victoria: "Yeah. Yeah, it's okay."

Peter: "What's your name, sir?"

Spirit Box — a young female voice cuts Peter off: "Horton."

There was a long pause as Paul fired up his camera, then ...

Spirit Box — shouting: "Alena!"

Spirit Box — a young female voice: "Oui?"

Peter: "Laila ...?"

Spirit Box — the same gruff male voice, shouting: "AAUGH!"

Spirit Box — a female voice with a French accent: "David."

Spirit Box — a young male yelled: "AAAIGH!"

Peter: "Laila, are you here?"

Spirit Box: "Go away!"

There are a pair of impact sounds, then ...

Spirit Box — the gruff, male voice, shouting: "Alena!"

Victoria: "I keep feeling like, vibrations on the floor, but that doesn't make any sense."

[The camera captures a male voice saying, "Danny."]

Peter: "The Spirit Box shouldn't be doing that much!"

Me: "No."

Victoria: "Anybody else feel vibrations in the floor?"

Peter: "No. Are you, Stephanie?"

Stephanie: "No."

Peter: "And you ... should be in line with those floor boards."

Victoria/Stephanie, looking down at themselves: "Yeah. Yeah."

Peter: "Ma'am, are you here with us in the room?"

Spirit Box — a female voice, cautiously: "No ..."

Spirit Box — a young or high-pitched elderly female voice: "Oh!"

Spirit Box — a male, matter-of-factly: "Doom."

Peter: "Yes ...?"

Spirit Box — a young male voice: "Uncle?"

Spirit Box — an older male, hesitant, slightly impatient-sounding: "Yes?"

Peter: "Please don't—"

Spirit Box — a high-pitched, young male voice: "Roger ...! Won't ya ...?"

Peter: "Please don't be afraid."

Spirit Box — a male voice, possible Scottish accent: "Take my niece."

Spirit Box — a female voice (punctuated by another blast of static): "Today?"

Victoria: "Someone appear?"

Spirit Box: A loud blast of dual-frequency static, like a shout.

Spirit Box — a male, sounding like a warning: "I mean it ...!"

Spirit Box: An identical loud blast of dual-frequency static, like a shout.

Peter: "Is Alexander with us?"

Paul, to Victoria and Stephanie: "What do you think?"

Spirit Box: A loud blast of dual-frequency static, like a shout.

Peter: "Is that him, yelling?"

Victoria: "Sounds like ..."

Peter: "Alexander?"

No reply.

Peter: "Is that your first name?"

No reply.

Peter: "Are you angry that we're here?"

Spirit Box — a male voice, confident: "I'll leave!"

Peter: "Pardon?"

Spirit Box — a male voice, abrupt: "No."

Spirit Box — a young female voice, clear and reassuring: "I'm not angry."

Spirit Box — a young male voice, possibly with a French or Spanish accent: "Don't go!"

Spirit Box, sound of a door slamming shut: "Wait!"

Peter: "Are you wondering why we're here?"

Spirit Box — a male voice, interrupting Peter: "No!"

Spirit Box — a burst of male-sounding static, shouting: "Alena!"

Spirit Box — a male voice: "We're leaving!"

Spirit Box — a young female voice: "AAIGH!"

Me: "How many people live in this house?"

There was a long pause and some breaks in the white noise static.

Me: "Can you tell me what year it is?"

Spirit Box — a low male voice heard under a high-pitched static blast: "Go away."

Paul: "Miriam. Ask for Miriam."

Spirit Box — a young female voice: "Go, bye … sweetheart!"

Paul: "I heard 'Miriam.'"

Spirit Box: "You didn't!"

Spirit Box: "Go down!"

Me: "Miriam?"

Spirit Box — young female voice: "Goodbye!"

Me: "Can you tell me what year it is, please?"

Spirit Box — a young female voice: "No!"

Spirit Box — a grumpy, older-sounding male voice, shouting: "Forget it!"

There was a long pause in the white noise static.

Me: "I heard that. I don't know."

Another long pause in the white noise static, then …

Spirit Box — a young, male-sounding voice: "Head home.…"

I turned the Spirit Box off. Instead of the team dispersing everyone remained in the room. Victoria was using the parabolic microphone.

I called for Miriam and asked, "There's a young gentleman that helps you. He's very nice; he wears glasses. Can you tell us his name, please?"

Immediately, static was heard through the parabolic microphone Victoria was pointing into the main-floor studio.

After a long pause, Paul asked, "Give us your last name?" Again, static interference "pulses" via the parabolic microphone immediately followed the question.

Peter asked, "Isabella, are you here instead?" All was quiet until more static from the parabolic microphone was heard.

I noted that I had placed my digital voice recorder on the wicker chair and it had turned off by itself.

"Isabella? Are you sitting in that chair?" Peter asked.

No reply.

"I beg your pardon, may I call you Isabella?" There were some crinkling sounds and a light knock that came from outside the northwest room.

"What the hell's moving out there?" I asked.

"Leaves blowing," Peter replied.

"That's not leaves," I stated.

"No. It's in here," Paul added.

"That's inside," I said, convinced of what I had heard.

"Plastic?" Peter noted.

"Yeah, it didn't sound like leaves to me," Victoria said.

"It wasn't. It was inside, right?" Paul said, moving to the doorway.

"Could be the plastic bag … crinkling," Peter said.

[The camera's audio captures a male voice, "Ya."

Male: "Henry."

Whispering.

There is a sound as if someone heavy is getting up from an old chair, with a squeak from wooden dowels.

Male voice: "Damn it."]

The team broke for lunch and prepared to leave the house for a local restaurant.

The audio/video surveillance systems were still operating and Peter left his digital voice recorder on the kitchen counter facing the front of the house. Peter closed the back door behind him.

"We don't have the key today so we have to have someone remain here," I stated.

Paul volunteered to stay behind.

We took his food order and headed out. Paul remained outside for about ten minutes.

[The main floor camera records a strange light moving up the wall along the stair banister.

Peter's digital voice recorder captures activity in the kitchen: A single hollow-sounding pop, movement culminating in a tap on the counter, then multiple pops, and ending with a sound like someone's arm falling to rest on a countertop.]

[The surveillance camera on the upper floor captures audio activity on its microphone as well as a shadow that moves quickly from the corner of the room toward the hallway. It then crosses the room toward the bathroom in front of the camera, and as it passes the camera there is a buzzing sound, like high-energy static. There is the sound of either small Christmas bells or bells on a cat's collar and then there is a bang next to the camera.]

Paul re-entered the house through the back door to warm up and remained in the kitchen, looking from time-to-time through the doorway into the studio.

Paul slammed the back door shut as he stepped outside again.

[Immediately in the upstairs bedroom there is heavy walking in the room, even though there is carpet, the footfalls sound like they are on hardwood]

[On Peter's digital voice recorder, there is a definite rustle of clothing followed by taps and more movement, close to the recorder, then away from it. Something is rattled; sounds like something toppling and wooden spoons rattling together. Like someone is searching through a kitchen cupboard.]

We arrived back at the house and found Paul waiting outside in the cold. Everyone entered the house. [Peter's digital recorder immediately captures a deep male voice yelling nothing but nonsense, sounding like "Yagobbity!"

A young woman or boy's voice follows, saying, "He'll go."]

On the upstairs camera there is a bright flash toward the camera. There is no one on that floor at the time.

The team spread out in the kitchen and dug into the food.

[The camera positioned by the front door captures audio sounding like either someone having sex or possibly that of someone giving birth.]

After lunch, the team moved off into the main floor, taking up positions in the various rooms. As Paul stood in the studio he saw someone outside.

"Somebody outside?" Paul called out.

"I don't know, why?" I asked.

"That window right there"— he indicated the southeast window — "something just passed, it looked black, going up the driveway to the back door," Paul said.

"Pete?"

"Yeah?" Peter replied from the kitchen.

"Anybody in the back?" I asked.

Peter looked out the kitchen window. "Don't see anything."

"It was black, like somebody wearing a black coat …?" Paul said.

"Could've been somebody," I said.

Peter went out to investigate. When he re-entered the house he reported that he hadn't see anyone outside.

Peter started activating and placing EM Pumps around the ground floor. (These pumps create a small electromagnetic field, which provide energy for spirits to manifest.)

Victoria reported feeling pressure in the northeast room, once the EM Pumps were activated, almost to the point of feeling dizzy.

Peter started turning the EM Pumps off one-by-one. As he did, he asked out loud, "Would anybody like to talk to us?"

[Peter's digital voice recorder gets a reply: "About what?"]

Victoria said, "I still feel pressure in my head."

Peter asked, "Is it as intense as it was before, with the boxes on, or ...?"

"Uh ... comes and goes. Not as intense as that, because I was feeling like, almost dizzy, but I definitely feel it across my forehead," Victoria reported.

I headed upstairs to check the surveillance system. As I knelt next to it, I saw a black orb approximately the size of a golf ball come out of thin air and spin past me before diving down into the floor and vanishing. The sight almost caused me to fall backwards and I scanned the room.

[The camera catches a black shadow dart from the small room and vanish down the stairs.]

I passed Peter heading upstairs alone with the parabolic microphone as I headed back down to the studio. Peter settled in the large northwest upstairs room.

Peter started asking questions. "Is there another male in the room with me?"

[Male voice on his digital recorder replies, "No."]

"Is there anybody upstairs with me?"

[A female throat-clearing sound is recorded.]

Peter noticed a chill envelop him from his spine outward as he sat against the northwestern-most corner of the room. He also recognized the possibility of a draft associated with sitting against an outer wall. However, this was the first time since he had been sitting against this wall that the cold had been felt.

After visiting the second-floor landing, then the smaller bedroom, Peter descended the stairs.

[With no one on the second floor the surveillance microphone records a male saying, "Baruba, Baruba." Its meaning unknown.

Then a male calling for "Henry."]

The team packed up and we called it a night. It would be a few days before we discovered what we had captured in our recordings.

Conclusions:

- It became evident to me that the spirits in the cottage were divided. One camp seemed friendly and willing to help and communicate with us. The other camp seemed aggressive toward us, and it appeared that they knew they had an upper hand on us as we were not able to see and/or hear them. It was as though they were taunting us.

- The property owners had told us that the place had never been investigated prior to us coming on-site; however, it seemed like some of these spirits were old hands at dealing with paranormal investigators, like they had been through this many times before. This certainly put me on guard.

4

PETER'S VISITS
JANUARY

Earning the trust of our clients is an incredible feeling, especially when we're dealing with so many unknown factors regarding the paranormal. Allowing otherwise total strangers free reign to investigate one's private property is not something most folks are willing to do.

After three worry-free investigations, the confidence of the property owners in our work — and in us as trustworthy people — continued unabated. This was certainly made apparent during the first two weeks of January.

Though the next formal investigation of the cottage property was scheduled to take place during the last week of January, the owner furnished us with a key and granted us access while they enjoyed a two-week vacation out-of-country.

Safety is Priority #1 to The Searcher Group; one of our team rules is that we never, ever, conduct an investigation alone. Because of this cardinal law, we now had a problem to overcome. Here was this tremendous opportunity to collect more data from this haunted location, but no one on the team was available to investigate until the end of the month. No one, that is, but Peter, the local boy.

Painfully aware of the safety procedures, Peter contacted me for advice regarding this dilemma. Ultimately, Peter talked me into agreeing that he should proceed with data-collecting experimentation, but he was to avoid the barn completely and to limit his visits to the cottage. Even then, Peter was to spend as little time alone inside as possible.

After great deliberation I gave authorization to proceed, albeit with caution. Peter immediately set to work on a plan of action. What follows are Peter's reports from his solo investigation.

Visit #1 — January 8

Arriving at the cottage before 8:00 p.m., I entered the silent building with my digital voice recorder already running and the E. Probe 1.0 pre-set at a high sensitivity detection level.

Since I was no longer a stranger to the spirits of the house, I thought I'd try to shake up their expectations a little by simply entering the cottage, offering the alarm device someone seemed to have a fondness for, then leaving without verbally acknowledging them or sharing my intent — a radical departure from normal Searcher Group procedure that "they" were no doubt becoming accustomed to.

Leaving the recorder on a chair in the dining room and the E. Probe 1.0 armed atop a drafting table far across the adjacent studio room, I locked the door behind me and drove away.

Returning two-and-a-half hours later, I couldn't help but grin widely as I emerged from my car. The alarm of the E. Probe could be heard blaring from inside the house, as it had done during previous investigations. Pleased with my success, I worked quickly, re-entering the house, deactivating the E. Probe, collecting the recorder, and moving toward the exit; again, without a word spoken.

As I stepped across the threshold of the cottage, I suddenly experienced an abrupt pressure change in my right ear — the most unpleasant kind of deafening, popping sensation one feels when travelling at high altitudes by airplane. I half-wondered if I had just been poked or punched by someone unseen as I locked the door behind me and returned to the safety of the car. The entire procedure took less than three minutes.

Turning the ignition, I broke my silence to tell the empty air that if I was being joined by a resident spirit at that moment, they were to remain behind and not follow me home. I also noted that for the first time since beginning investigation of the property, I could smell traces of the air freshener scent from the interior of the cottage inside the car. This familiar odour lingered for about a minute as I drove away, dissipating completely as I passed the local cemetery.

The perceived success of the night's experiment was short-lived as I began analyzing the audio data. Seven minutes and fifty-one seconds after I had left the cottage, the E. Probe 1.0 began alarming and — unfortunately — remained alarmed for the rest of the recording. Instead of a successful ghostly interaction, it seemed that the device had simply malfunctioned and its incessantly-loud blare drowned out any possible EVPs that may have occurred.

Visit #2 — January 10

I rarely drive anywhere listening to music or the radio. So it was on this evening that minutes after leaving home, I began hearing the ear-splitting E. Probe 1.0 alarm in my head. Glancing down at the device lying quietly on the passenger seat beside me, I noted the "ghost" of the alarm sound resonating in my inner ears lasted fifteen to twenty seconds before giving way to the normal ambiance of evening traffic outside the car.

I can honestly say I had not heard the pure alarm sound of the device for more than twenty-four hours before this spontaneous, ear-ringing phenomenon and I haven't heard a similar ear-ringing since. The irony that this occurred on my way to the second solo data-collecting experiment was not lost on me.

Deciding to once again remain silent after entering the cottage, I placed the digital recorder inside the alcove at the base of the staircase to the second floor, the microphone pointed into the open studio beyond. Dropping the sensitivity of the E. Probe 1.0 to a lower setting* than the previous visit, I placed the device on the seat of the wicker chair in the northwest room, confirmed the recorder was operating properly, and exited the house silently, without incident.

[*In order to activate the alarm of the E. Probe 1.0 at this setting, a source of electrical energy would need to approach within 3 millimetres of the device's aerial.]

Two hours and forty minutes later, I returned to the cottage to retrieve the equipment and was not smiling when I stepped from the car to hear the alarm blaring from inside the building again. Praying this evening's recording would reveal this alarm was actually one of several, I quickly collected the equipment and exited the cottage.

While I consider it a victory whenever the alarm is activated by an unseen force, unfortunately, once activated (this time, nine minutes and forty-seven seconds after my departure), the alarm remained on for the duration of this recording, as well.

Looking on the positive side, at the very least I was slowly determining the increments of the device's ideal sensitivity setting. Still, it came at the cost of potential EVP loss, so a new tack was definitely in order.

I learned something else that evening, as well. Wearing the same clothes I wore during the first night and spending the identical amount of time inside the cottage both times this evening, I could not detect the air freshener scent inside my car after exiting.

Visit #3 — January 12–13

On my way out of town for another investigation, I stopped by the cottage at 3:00 p.m. to introduce the next component of my experiments — a pair of powder traps.

Ensuring the surface of my target areas was as close to flat as possible, I secured flattened garbage bags to the floor of the mid-way staircase landing with tape before sprinkling a generous amount of flour, covering the entire area in a half-inch blanket of solid whiteness from corner-to-corner. Stepping over the staircase trap, I repeated this process on garbage bags taped flat to the linoleum floor just inside the entrance to the second-floor bathroom — another location of intense paranormal activity. I remained silent the whole time I worked.

Taking several control photos of both traps, I exited the cottage and continued on my way.

Hours later, a thick fog greeted me as I returned to the property at 1:00 a.m., setting the scene for a perfect Hollywood horror event. Though no figures emerged, arms outstretched, from the walls of the fog, I was sufficiently creeped out by the ambience to make this visit a quick one.

Checking the powder traps for signs of footprints or powder disturbance, I noted with some disappointment there was no change in either. Accompanying my digital recorder this time was my E. Probe 2.0 alarm device — an upgrade model with a pre-set sensitivity and a much quieter alarm. Both were placed apart from each other and activated on the main floor before I exited the cottage.

I returned twelve hours later to retrieve the equipment, by the warm light of the sun. The powder traps were clean, the E. Probe 2.0 was still armed and the digital recorder had stopped itself, as the memory card was full, containing almost nine hours of audio data.

Review of the recording revealed a few noteworthy elements. Unbeknownst to me, a heavy rainfall occurred during the wee hours of the morning and it was during this tempest that the recorder picked up what sounded like hard, pounding footfalls stomping back and forth between the recorder on the main floor and the farthest reaches of the second-storey, on multiple occasions. When the intensity of the downpour weakened, the pounding ceased; if the rain began to intensify, the running thumps would resume in uneven patterns.

Recalling the theory that electricity produced by falling water may "feed" spirits with energy enough to manifest detectable activity, could this heavy rainfall have acted as a catalyst for what was recorded?

Subsequent questioning of the homeowner revealed that while the building does not have a sump pump installed, there is a water pump connected with the unused well, located just out back of the cottage. Though the first conclusion to jump to is the sound of the water pump being activated by the excessive downpour, it does not explain the random growing and fading intensities of the pounding toward and away from the recorder; that and the fact that not even the homeowner had heard such intense pounding while working inside the cottage on rainy days.

Visit #4 — January 15

On this evening, wind chimes were introduced to the mix, hung from a nail on the studio wall. The digital recorder was once again placed in the staircase alcove and the E. Probe 1.0 — this time adjusted to its lowest sensitivity set-ting — was placed on a chair in the northwest room. If someone really wished to activate the alarm, they would need to grip the aerial tightly to do so.

Retrieving the equipment three hours and twenty-one minutes later, I was surprised to discover the normally reliable digital recorder registered "Low Battery" and could not be turned off, no matter what I tried, which was a first. Checking the powder traps before exiting, I noted they had not been disturbed.

Arriving back home and entering the house with the equipment in my arms, I looked down in time to see a button on the recorder being pressed, as by a pen cap, causing the recorder to spring back to life! The battery now indicated "Half Power" and the whole unit returned to function normally.

Review of the recording revealed neither the wind chimes nor the E. Probe 1.0 had been moved or alarmed, however it was interesting to note that the recording stopped itself the very second I am heard unlocking the back door of the cottage. As noted earlier, this recorder has the capacity to store almost nine hours of data. Was this pure coincidence, a random malfunction or perhaps someone taking one last "suck" of energy from the recorder just before I walked in? If the latter, was I to derive a message from this action?

Visit #5 — January 16

By 7:48 p.m. I was back in the car jotting notes on this evening's experi-ment. Tonight I introduced a pad of paper and a charcoal pencil as well as a Pop-O-Matic die bubble to the cottage. The recorder (loaded with fresh batteries) was left on the kitchen counter pointed toward the studio and the E. Probe 1.0 (now adjusted one notch higher than its lowest sensitivity setting) was left in the smallest room across from the second-floor staircase.

I silently demonstrated how to shake the die up by pressing the plastic bubble and allowing the die to come to a full rest before repeating this action several more times for the benefit of anyone observing me. I left the die at the number 4, checked the powder traps, and took several photos before exiting.

I detected traces of the familiar cottage air freshener scent around me upon entering the car, but this dissipated quickly and did not remain.

By the time I returned three hours later, I decided the silent treatment I was trying to maintain had lost any effectiveness it may have ever had on the unseen residents of the cottage. After all, how were the ghosts to know what I was expecting of them for my recordings if I didn't ask them to do something? Gathering up the recorder and the E. Probe 1.0, I respectfully invited whoever was listening to convey a message back to me using the paper and pencil, the powder, or by shifting the die to a number that held some significance to them, before leaving for the night.

Reviewing the recording of this evening revealed some intriguing phenomena: several knocking sounds were captured, smaller taps and a single, loud footfall. But what made this recording even more unique was the multiple number of times the die bubble — or something that sounded similar — was popped without changing the top-face of the die (the number 4) or shifting it from its resting place inside the plastic bubble. In other words, what I kept hearing was an imitation of the actual distinct popping sound.

As for the message that I broke my silence to ask for, I believe I received it loud and clear a few short hours later.

January 17, 1:25 a.m.

For the record, I am not an avid dreamer. I'm sure I do dream, but like many people, I forget the majority of them the moment I awake.

Crawling into bed at a ridiculously late hour, I quickly found myself falling into blissful sleep. What seemed like a matter of minutes later, between the stages of being fully awake and in deep sleep, inside what I could best describe as my "mind's eye," I perceived an adult male standing over me, next to my side of the bed. Wasting no time, the figure leaned forward and shouted, "PETER ROE!" like a drill sergeant.

In a foggy-minded delirium, I bolted upright and swung my legs off the side of the bed, ready to respond obediently, replying, "Yes? What?"

The lack of a response made me realize I was speaking to no one. Thankfully, my knee-jerk reply wasn't loud and abrupt enough to wake my wife. While still cognitive of this extraordinary occurrence and the fact that it was significant enough to remember, I took note of the time but was still too tired to feel afraid. I returned to the warmth of our comforter and fell into a deep sleep.

Visit #6 — January 19

Recalling the team's astounding success during the second investigation, I decided to try my own daytime experiment beginning at 10:30 a.m. I placed the recorder on an easel in the studio, the mic pointed toward the open door to the kitchen, beyond. Adjusting the E. Probe 1.0 one notch higher than the last visit, I set that down on the windowsill of the small room at the top of the stairs.

There were no powder disturbances, no markings of charcoal pencil on the pad of paper, no movement of the bubble die, and no residual household odours followed me to the car. Though I addressed the house politely before exiting, I was careful not to empower anyone listening by acknowledging the strange event of a couple days' previous.

By 1:37 p.m., I was back in the car, having retrieved the recorder and E. Probe 1.0. I had arrived to find the alarm was once again blaring and — though it was placed across the length of the cottage and upstairs — had ruined a third recording by drowning out the sounds of the building. Upon analysis, this time someone touched off the alarm nearly sixteen minutes after I had left the cottage. Again, there were no powder, pencil, or die changes.

The positive aspect of this experiment was that I had finally found "the sweet spot" on the alarm for this location.

Visit #7 — January 23

The window for my solo data-collecting was closing fast. I returned to the cottage at my first opportunity, at 7:39 p.m., eager to try another new tactic.

Checking the powder traps, paper pad, and die bubble to find there were still no changes in any of them, I addressed the house good-naturedly and pointed out that the opportunity to communicate with me alone was rapidly coming to an end, politely saying that no more interested parties would be available to hear their concerns after The Searcher Group was finished visiting with them.

Moving to the Pop-O-Matic bubble, I depressed it to shake up the die several times, and each time I did so, I enthusiastically called out the number that came up.

I reasoned based on the imitation popping sounds that had been recorded during Visit #5, that perhaps if a new "norm" of shouting out the appropriate numbers was introduced, then perhaps whoever was imitating the popping sound might follow suit and shout the numbers they "saw" or imagined were coming up, as well (and be recorded, doing so). It was a long shot, but worth trying.

Analysis of the three-hour recording turned up some interesting results. There were several more imitation die-popping sounds, but no numbers were called out after each 'pop,' as I had demonstrated. The recorder, which had been placed on the window shared between the dining room and the kitchen, picked up subtle metallic jingling noises quite close to it. This jingling resembled a nearby charm bracelet more than a set of keys being shaken or several coins clinking together.

January 25, 12:20 a.m.

In hindsight, perhaps my requests for communication with the residents of the cottage were truly answered, only they were not to be on my terms.

Apart from the bizarre mid-sleep occurrence of January 17, what happened on this morning made me reconsider what I would otherwise have chalked up to exhaustion and an overactive imagination.

Deciding to go to bed at another ridiculous work-week hour, I sauntered along the half-lit hallway toward our bedroom. Light streamed into the dark of the hall from the bathroom on the left, revealing the dim outlines of the spare room door and our daughter's bedroom door, opposite.

As I took two or three steps forward, a loud snap suddenly emanated from the threshold of the spare room doorway — mere feet away. Within a second of the sound, my instinct was to freeze in my tracks and look toward its source. As I did so, I caught a hint of a shadow at least five feet high flitting from the spare room door toward the lit, half-closed bathroom, before all was still.

The environment surrounding me felt as if I was in the presence of someone else. The abrupt snap of the laminate flooring sounded as if someone had been standing in the doorway of the spare room and when they realized I was approaching, took their weight off that place to launch themselves into the bathroom, six feet away.

Did my daughter get up to use the washroom? Was my wife around the corner of the spare room, hiding for some reason? I waited for a short time to listen for movement, before asking after my daughter. No reply came and I continued forward a little more cautiously, telling myself it was a ridiculous notion that she would be awake at that time of morning. Still, I peered into the darkened spare room, then slowly opened the bathroom door the rest of the way to inspect the interior.

In the six years we have lived in our house, I have walked that hall hundreds of times. Never once have I heard a floorboard creak or snap like this, simply by walking the same path I was routinely walking as I was that morning.

I climbed into bed cautiously, listening for more foreign sounds in and outside the bedroom. Satisfied my alarm clock was set for the correct wake-up time, I slowly relaxed under the covers.

What seemed like a short time later, my bedside alarm clock sounded, its merciless beeping alerting me that it was time to rise for the day and begin it by preparing lunch for our daughter's school day, as was my weekday custom. Crediting the incredible sense of exhaustion I was feeling as a result of my late turn-in time, I staggered to the kitchen and began to start the day.

About fifteen minutes passed as I fed the cats, washed a few dishes, and started to make coffee. While I was filling the kettle with water, I turned to reach for the stove element dial. My eyes fell on the stovetop clock. The digital clock read 3:48.

I blinked, utterly perplexed. Rubbing my eyes, I focused again on the stovetop clock, before glancing to the microwave clock, which echoed the display panel of the stove's.

Ensuring I hadn't turned on any electrical equipment during my time in the kitchen, I returned to bed, grateful for another two hours' worth of sleep. An inspection of my bedside clock confirmed it was indeed still set to alarm at 5:55 a.m.

Events such as these had never happened to me before, nor have they happened since.

None of the at-home incidents I've described would strike me as particularly frightening or thought-provoking on their own, but the fact that they occurred within a space of a few early morning hours after I had requested communication during my solo investigations, compels me to include them here.

Must I attribute them all as products of an overactive imagination, or to a mind trained to perceive them with open skepticism? Could I have been paid a visit or two by a resident of the cottage, boldly investigating me?

Be careful what you wish for.

Conclusions:

It was interesting to note over the time Peter commenced his solo visits to the cottage that the non-aggressive posture produced little results. However there seemed to be some sort of bond developed over this time as a spirit in the building started following him home.

This raised a red flag for me. Sometimes when they follow you home it is to disrupt your household, a sort of retaliation to investigating theirs.

5

THIRD INVESTIGATION
LATE JANUARY

The team assembled slowly, and as we waited for the rest to show up Peter, Paul, and I looked over the cottage exterior. It was bitter cold and Paul suggested we move inside just as the rest of the team pulled into the driveway. We headed inside and placed our equipment in the kitchen.

Paul and I started to set up the audio and video surveillance equipment. Joan, our medium for the night, toured the main floor, checking each room and paying close attention to the northwest room and the alcove under the stairs.

One of the investigators, James, started to take photos while Peter and Victoria prepared their equipment.

Joan returned and mentioned that she had received an impression of a body buried on the property and that it was hidden, possibly in the barn.

Peter and Joan headed to the second floor. Victoria followed them up.

They moved through the second floor and stopped at the bathroom.

"This house is very old. There was a husband and wife and he had a daughter," Joan began.

"Here? Up here or in the house, generally?" Peter inquired, looking for clarity.

"No, generally, yeah. They lived here, the three of them. Maybe they had a son, I don't know, it's … I feel like the husband is abusing her or just shouting at her and putting her inside that — under the stairs. And there was a lock; he used to lock it. And that was a hiding place for her; a place she had to be," Joan explained.

"So he put her in there for punishment? Or did she have to hide from him in there?" Peter asked.

"Both. Sometimes she went there and sometimes he had to put her there for a while."

Joan was indicating the alcove built under the stairs on the main floor.

"It was that spot that you were looking in earlier downstairs?"

"Yeah. As soon as I opened it I knew there was a child in there, or used to be there. And as soon as I opened it and it was like … there was a connection. I knew that. I don't know if it's a 'he' or a 'she.' Before I came here I told Richard that I feel like there is a husband and wife and a child."

Peter didn't say anything. Later, he suggested that the child was a tomboy, which would explain the medium's confusion.

"So are these feelings you're picking up, or can they share names and dates with you yet?" Peter asked.

"I don't know, yet. I told Richard it's like people are coming to this house and going; it's like neighbours or they're doing something here. Lots of people. I see people — they are coming and leaving. Lots of noises — talking about things. I don't know yet."

"Is anybody here with us, now?" Peter asked.

"No. Here? No."

"Like the angry man?"

"Actually, downstairs in that northwest room — the second one. The chair I was sitting down in, I felt like a male used to sit there. And I sat down on a chair; I felt like he doesn't want me to sit there. I felt there was a guy; he used to sit in that corner, always."

"And that's the same angry man, or perhaps a different guy?" Peter asked.

"He's not angry, but I think he's drinking a lot, like, getting drunk most of the time and I can see that his right hand is like that." Joan mimed pounding up and down. "I don't know what he has in his hand, I don't see it; I don't feel it yet, but … he has a cane or something in his hand."

"So while he was drunk he would be angry?"

"Yeah, he wants something. He's shouting and he wants it. That's why everybody gets scared or something? I feel like it's not a happy house, at all. I don't feel happy. It's like lonely. It feels so weird."

Joan opened the closet just outside the master bedroom. "It's like the wife used to put something in here. They had a baby, also…"

"In addition to the other child?" Peter inquired, looking into the closet.

"Yeah. It's like, uh … baby stuff. But there's no baby; I don't feel any baby" — she paused — "Maybe passed away, or something? Someone died in the bathroom."

Paul and I arrived to set up a surveillance camera in the adjacent room.

"Yeah, it's a female."

"Young? Older?" Peter asked.

"Not young, not old. Fifty … No, younger than that. It's not the first time she gets the pain. It's so many times."

"What kind of pain? Where does it originate?"

"She's bleeding."

"From her body? Her head?"

"It's from … her face. I feel like it's the face and she has a pain here." Joan indicated her abdominal area then paused, pushing aside the shower curtains. "No, someone was abusing her. It's her husband."

"The same one from downstairs?"

"That guy, yeah. That's the one. They had the daughter or son; I don't know, yet. It'd get scared, go downstairs and go to the little place."

"Uh hm. Under the stairs?"

"Yeah."

[The surveillance camera microphone captures a child saying, "Get back momma."

A male voice comes over the microphone: "Oh oh."

The child calls out, "Dad," sobbing and sounding frightened.

Then there was a very loud big bang.]

"So it sounds like she is dying or died of complications from the abuse. Beatings, or something like that, finally killed her?" Peter summarized.

"She kills herself, I think. It's so complicated. I can see the pain and every time she comes here … washes … and changes her clothes and goes. I can hear crying and this door was closed and she's sitting here." Joan sits on the edge of the bathtub. "And she's just crying. She has black hair. She's so worried about the things, I don't know. This is the place she used to come most of the time."

"Like a retreat? A safe haven?"

"She closed that door and locked it."

"Do you think she eventually died in this room?" Peter inquired.

"I can see a woman is lying down here" — indicating the bathtub — "and the head is here" — indicating opposite the taps — "but I don't know. She doesn't move, but I can see her; she's sitting here, also. I can see she's not moving at all … and it's bleeding."

"Is there water in there too, with her, or is it just her?"

"She was just with the blood."

"From her head?"

Leaving the rest of the team, Paul and I went downstairs. I was whistling. *[The microphone records a child humming along.]*

Paul turned the upstairs light on from the bottom of the stairs. *[A child yells, "No."]*

[An older male says, "Hell." And then calls out, "Danny."
Kid hums again.]

"She has a pain from her tummy. I don't know what happened; I can feel it. And she's bleeding here, also. I cannot see if she took her life or … if someone killed her."

"She has no energy left. She just want to … oh … send off."

Joan stood inside the bathtub, touching the fixtures and pushing back the curtains. "She used to cry here."

She lifted a small toy black cat figurine lodged in the soap/shampoo rack and said, "They had a daughter. Yeah, it was a daughter, not a son. I can feel her now." Joan replaced the cat figurine then stepped out of the bathtub, looking up to the ceiling panel leading to the roof. "She used to hide something up there. She used to come up here like this … and put it on the right side … and put something there, in this area."

"Something she didn't want her husband to know about, perhaps? That's the only thing I can think of. I mean, if she's abused and needs to retreat here … she'd … put something up there?" Peter said.

"She has some kind of … like a weapon, or a knife, or something sharp, and she's just putting it there. And she's locking that door every time. I can see her, locking and locking. She comes here and she wants to do it and she's just moving like this," — Joan made frustrated stabbing gestures — "and talking to herself. And she goes up there and just put it there" — she pauses — "And … then … cleans up and goes outside, again. But the child — why I see her lying down. Dead, or just lying … Yeah, she's not moving."

"This is the same person — I was just thinking — that you felt sitting there and also lying there; maybe there's the possibility that there are two people?"

Joan said she had to "go to that place again," meaning the alcove under the stairs, so she and Peter exited the bathroom. Before they left, Joan examined and turned the doorknob a few times, saying the half that was inside the bathroom needed replacing. She jiggled it and said, "He's trying to open it."

On the way out of the master bedroom, Joan stopped and examined the air vent by the doorway and commented, "This other person's daughter or someone — they are listening from somewhere. The sound goes down."

She returned to the closet just outside the master bedroom and said, "She used to put something in here. What is it? Baby's furniture, or something." She illustrated the woman/mother bending over the upper banister to call for her daughter.

"How old would the daughter be, you think? Roughly?" Peter asked.

"I can see like eight years old…. Seven/eight."

On the ground floor, Joan asked to be locked under the stairs for a short time then let out again. She confirmed that the daughter was thrown under there for punishment.

Paul and I met up on the main floor. *[The camera's audio records a male's voice calling out some type of warning, saying, "Get back."]*

There were physical sounds coming from the northwest room and both Paul and I checked the room but found nothing.

"We are going out to the barn to look for a body," Paul yelled out.

[Although we do not hear it, a male yells, "Alright." And then calls for "Miriam."]

Paul called out, "Come out!"

[Male yells, "Hey." Followed by whispers which cannot be understood.]

James arrived on the main floor from the second floor. "We heading out?" he asked.

"Going to the barn," I told him.

Paul, James, and I headed outside, planning our tactic in the barn.

[On the camera's microphone there are odd sounds like things being moved, tapping sounds, and whispers, then the older male calls out, "Richard."]

Peter, Joan, and Victoria joined us outside and we all headed to the barn together.

As Victoria, James, Paul, and I descended into the barn cellar, Joan showed Peter an empty knife sheath nailed to the southern wall of the barn. "Remember I told you she was hiding something? She took it from here. That's the thing; whatever it was, I don't know. It's like a knife, or something. That's why … you can find it up there in the attic."

We later spoke to the owner about this knife sheath and she confirmed it held an asparagus knife and that it was in use in the present-day kitchen.

"Yeah, it does look pretty old. I'm not sure if the current owners put that there or …"

"It looks like it's been nailed there, so I don't think it can come off. Can it?" Peter said, examining the sheath.

"Yeah, I just took it out, just a few minutes ago."

"The whole nail, right?" Peter asked.

"No." Joan slid the sheath off the nail. *[Immediately there is a loud blast of static captured on the digital voice recorder Peter is holding, followed by the sound of a female panting.]*

Peter followed Joan down into the barn cellar.

"We need to talk to the owner to see if we can do a little digging in here, right here," Paul stated, kicking the dirt on the mound.

Peter asked, "How are you doing, Joan?"

She laughed and said, "It's too much in here!"

"What do you mean, too much?"

"I don't know, it's … it's him and he's doing something here."

"The same guy from the house?" Peter asked.

"Same guy, yeah. This guy's … his age I can see is like … forty-eight … forty-nine … and he has a moustache. Beard … not that much but you can see just a little bit and he's, uh … he's actually tall. When he walks here, he is like, walking very fast." She demonstrated the man's gait.

Paul started hacking at the mound of raised soil on the cellar floor with a pitchfork he'd been handed, but stopped after determining the frost was too hard at this point in time.

"Why don't we go up and I'll lay this powder," Paul suggested.

[Peter's digital voice recorder captures a male voice saying, "No!"]

Paul and I headed upstairs. Paul started to lay some powder traps as I took random interior photos. Victoria remained in the cellar conducting an EVP session.

Peter and Joan followed us up and started to poke around the storage area between the stalls and the current owner's metal-shop. Joan stated, "He's hiding."

"In here?" Peter asked.

"It's like, in this area. He's not showing himself; I don't know why. Why he died? He … he's …" Joan trailed off.

Paul headed up the ladder to the loft and started taking a series of photos of the loft, sort of a panoramic series of pictures.

"Do you think he died on the property or came back? Died in the hospital or something and then … came back here?" Peter asked.

"I don't know; I don't feel it. I just see him.… There is another man, also; there's an older one. And now I am confused. Here, that guy is young; not that young but, like, forty-seven or something. That guy is a little bit older. How come … they live together, or.… He's doing something downstairs, this tall guy. That one is not this one; these are different."

"Could be different times, maybe? Different levels of time, maybe?" Peter asked.

"I think so, yes. I feel he has someone downstairs — in that place we were? They are doing something together. They're working. Of course they fight sometimes. Like, verbally."

"Man it's cold. Let's head back and warm up," I suggested.

The team started to head back to the cottage.

Paul stopped at the barn door. "Who the frig is this guy?" he said out loud, staring at his camera display screen.

The team gathered around for a look as Paul thumbed through the photos: loft, loft, loft, boy's face, loft, loft.

The boy looked like something out of the 1960s, with a wavy haircut and thick black-rimmed glasses. But who was he? We were unable to explain how Paul got this photo. I had never seen anything like it before.

As we moved across the property toward the cottage, James stopped at the barn door with Joan.

"I saw the door close slowly and it did not make a sound." He demonstrated by moving the door open and closed. Each movement brought a loud, drawn-out squeak. "I don't understand how it moved without a sound."

[At that moment his digital recorder captures the sound of a child playing.]

James and Joan hurried to catch up to the rest of us and we all entered the warmth of the cottage.

Joan felt the boy from the barn was named Mark. It was my experience that nothing was that easy and I knew this was going to take a great deal of investigation to discover who the boy was.

I headed upstairs to check on the surveillance system. Peter and Victoria checked on the E. Probe as it had been activated in our absence. Joan moved back into the studio, again looking at the small door under the stairs. The rest wandered, taking random photos.

Peter came into the living room and started looking through some old photos.

[A male voice is captured saying, "Pictures."]

Peter put the photos back into his kit and met up with Joan. "So are you sensing many people coming and going here?" he asked.

"Not upstairs, but here on the main floor I do. It's like they're neighbours or … family members and they're coming and going."

"A lot of them all at once?"

"No, not all together coming; it's like this door is always open for everyone." Joan turned toward the east wall, where the original entranceway was. "It's like that…. Doing their business, or something."

Peter knew the area she had indicated was the original entry; now a wall with a bay window in it, and that all these people coming and going could very well be Parishioners coming to church. None of which Joan was aware of.

The team assembled and headed upstairs to try a Spirit Box session.

After operating the system for seventeen minutes without any success, Peter suggested we look at the attic hatch located in the second-floor bathroom.

He climbed up on the edge of the bathtub and put his hand into the hatch, feeling around, but found nothing but insulation.

James came forward and reported that there were several instances where he wanted to take a picture using the flash on his camera, but the flash did not work for several pictures in a row and then started working again.

This happened in every room of the house with the exception of the upstairs hallway and the small bedroom upstairs.

Peter, Joan, and Victoria settled in the northwest room. Peter placed his digital voice recorder on the wicker chair and then drew out his pendulum and attempted to make communication. (The pendulum can allow for yes or no answers.)

Peter asked, "Isabella, are you here? Am I sitting on you?"

The pendulum started to rotate clockwise, indicating yes.

"Isabella, are you here?"

[On his digital voice recorder a very subtle sounding female voice says what sounds like, "Here I am."]

"Is this you?"

The pendulum indicated no.

"Are you a male? Is this a male spirit I'm speaking to?"

Pendulum: small yes.

"Are you Jonathan?"

Pendulum: swings up and down, neutral.

"Are you Alexander? Is this Alexander I'm speaking with?"

Pendulum: neutral.

"Does it bother you that we're in the house with you?"

Pendulum: wide arching yes.

"Does it disturb you that we're here with you?"

Pendulum: wide arching yes.

"Would you like us to leave?"

Pendulum: an ever growing indication of yesses.

"Do we make you angry?"

Pendulum: large yes.

"Are you Alexander?"

Pendulum: large yes.

"Alexander, I don't know if you can help me answer the question, but why was this building moved from its original place?

"I understand and I know you can't answer my question with a yes or no, but I do hope you're speaking to me at the same time because the device next to me should be able to hear you. Do you understand that?"

Pendulum: yes.

"Do you understand that I might be able to hear you if you're speaking to me?"

Pendulum: yes, but slowing down.

"Would you like us to stay?"

Pendulum: slowing down.

"Would you like us to stay longer?"

Pendulum: swings up and down, into neutral.

"Would you like us to stay longer, Alexander?"

Pendulum: no.

"You would like us to leave."

Pendulum: no.

"Alexander, are you still with me?"

Pendulum: swings up and down, neutrally.

"Am I speaking with somebody else, now? Clockwise for 'yes,' counter-clockwise for 'no.'"

From outside the room Paul reported that the static field detector was going off and on.

Peter continued, "Are you afraid to speak?"

Pendulum: swings up and down, neutrally.

"Why are you afraid? Are there secrets here?"

Pendulum: swings up and down, neutrally.

"Are there secrets that surround this cottage? This building? You can speak to me."

Peter continued, "We only seek the truth. Are you a truthful person?"

Pendulum: yes.

"You are a truthful person, are you?"

There was the sound of an exhale.

"Do you fear God?"

Pendulum: large yes.

"Is this why you stay? Because you fear God?"

Pendulum: yes.

"Did you do something that God would not approve of when you were alive?"

Pendulum: yes.

"What did you do? Kill?"

Pendulum: yes.

"Did you kill someone with a pistol?"

Pendulum: yes, but slowing down.

"You shot someone?"

Pendulum: small yes.

"Did someone shoot themselves accidentally with your gun?" *[Immediately after this question the digital recorder captures whispers, what sounds like a female saying, "Yes," and then something indistinguishable.]*

"And you feel responsible?"

Pendulum: growing yes.

"Do you remember the name of the person who was shot?"

[A female voice says clearly, "Sam Maclean."]

"Can you shout it at me, please?"

The pendulum swings broadly, colliding with Peter's upturned left palm, interrupting its momentum. "Who was shot? Shout their name, please! What is your name, please?"

Pendulum: large yes.

"God knows where you are. You can't hide from him. You can confess your sins to us. We're the only ones who will listen to you right now, do you know that?"

Pendulum: yes but slowing.

"If you tell us the truth and you are a truthful person like you say you are, then you have nothing to fear."

Pendulum: small yes.

[There is a slight exhale captured on the recorder.]

"Do you understand that? We're not here to judge you."

Pendulum: small yes.

"We're here to help you. Do you need help?"

Pendulum: small yes.

"Then you need to give us some information, please."

Pendulum: small yes.

"Am I still speaking with Alexander?"

Pendulum: slowing down

[A light male whisper: "Maybe."]

"This is not Alexander?"

Pendulum: swings up and down, neutrally.

"Am I still speaking to a male?"

Pendulum: swings neutral.

"Female?"

Pendulum: swings neutral.

Peter continued his communication attempts. "Are you still a truthful person?"

Pendulum: swings neutral but with more power behind it.

"That's not yes or no."

Pendulum: swings neutral.

"Are you just having fun with me?"

Pendulum: immediately changes direction and indicates no.

"No what? You don't want me to leave?"

Pendulum: no.

"You understand we could try to help you?"

Pendulum: no.

"You don't think we can help you?"

Pendulum: no.

"Really?"

Pendulum: slowing down fast.

"Do you think there's even a slight chance we could help you?"

Pendulum: slowing down, bobbing neutrally.

"Do you think there is a slight chance we could help you?"

Pendulum: yes.

As Peter winded down the pendulum session, Joan said there was a female energy on his left side.

Peter admitted feeling a patch of coldness.

"She was standing; she was putting a hand on the chair; she was just looking at that, indicating the pendulum."

"Would you like me to leave, ma'am?"

Pendulum: small yes and slowing.

"Do you understand that we come here and ask questions because we think we might be able to help you?"

Pendulum: stops all movement.

"Is this Isabella next to me?"

Pendulum: no movement at all.

"She's gone," Joan reported.

Paul and I were up on the second floor doing an EVP session. All seemed quiet, but as we headed for the stairs, there was a very loud bang behind us. We both spun around, not knowing what to expect, but there was nothing there. It sounded like two large bamboo sticks slamming together.

Victoria opened the door under the stairs and moved inside the space, sitting, trying to coax the child into communicating.

[There is a female-sounding cry or whine captured on Peter's digital recorder.]

Our technical manager, John Mullan, had built several static field detectors and I felt I should set one up in the northwest room as an experiment.

Peter entered the room and asked, "Alexander, you like your whiskey?" The static detector glowed brighter. "That's it! Come closer to the blue light. Don't be afraid of me, please. That's great."

Peter reported he was getting major goose bumps. The light became brighter. "Thank you!"

Peter reported he felt gooseflesh on his left side as he stood across the room from the static detector.

"Are you going to stay there if I walk over to join you?" Peter asked as he took a few paces forward. The light turned off then started glowing again. Peter started forward again, but after one step the light went off completely. He took a step back and the light returned. He took a step forward and the light died. He stepped back and the light returned. He took two steps to his right and stopped: No change in the light. He stepped forward toward the front window and the light began to dim and blink off, but remained on. Peter offered to shake hands, took a step toward the corner, and stretched his right arm closer. The static detector light died. Peter kept his hand outstretched without getting any closer.

"Is this your corner? Can you touch me on the hand, at least? I promise I won't go any closer to you, but … can you pull one of my fingers or something, please?" There was a long pause while nothing happened. "I can't grab you; I can't touch you. Maybe you think I can."

Peter asked Joan to assist him. She entered the room just as James and Victoria moved to the doorway.

"I feel like there's someone there. I just want to shake their hand," Peter said.

"Yeah. It's in that corner, sitting down," Joan reported.

"But I feel like its growing, this area; I used to be able to get a lot closer to it."

"So don't turn it off until I come there, okay? Don't do that. Just leave it on." Joan hunched down and slowly approached the northwest corner in a non-threatening manner. The light stayed lit.

"You could get closer than I could!" Peter said from the doorway.

Still approaching the corner, slowly, Joan said, "Leave it."

"Yeah, it's here. I feel it, here," Joan said, settling a few feet away from the corner.

"Male? Female?" Peter inquired.

"Female. It's just so interesting. The female is in this area" — she indicated the northwest corner. "The male always in that area" — she indicated the opposite corner. "I don't know why. She's here; she's upstairs."

Peter demonstrated his effect on the light intensity for Victoria and James as he addressed the corner of the room: "Can you stay on for Joan? Look! It stays on! She's even touching the table and it remained lit."

"Do you not want Peter near you?" Victoria asked.

[The digital recorder captures a voice saying, "No."]

"She's scared," Joan stated.

"She's scared of me?" Peter asked.

"She's scared of men."

"Is this Isabella?"

"What? I'm sensing Angela. Who is that?" Joan seemed confused.

"Okay, Angela, can you tell us your last name, please?" Peter asked.

Joan in concentration: "Davidson."

"What year is it, please?"

"Eighty-four?" The detector light started dimming.

"Don't go! No, don't go!"

The detector light died.

"She's gone?" Peter said, upset.

"Yeah, she'll come back," Joan said.

The static detector brightened, meaning the spirit was returning.

"There she is. Angela?"

"Don't ask too many questions, she says. She doesn't want to answer."

"Is there someone here who will? In the house?" Peter asked.

"She says lots of people!" Joan said, amused.

"Lots of people who will answer questions?"

"Lots of people are here."

"Are they all people who have lived here before?" Victoria asked.

"Yes. Everybody's here," Joan stated.

"Do you all see each other?" Victoria asked.

"She doesn't like some of them."

"How long did you live here, Angela?"

"Fifty … fifty …"

There was a whine sound, wooooo.

"Okay, I won't touch. You want to leave?" Joan said.

"Do you want me to leave? I'm going!" Peter said, walking away from the room.

"She left?" Victoria asked.

"No, she's here! Peter, come back!" Joan called out.

"Is there something that she wants to tell us?" Victoria asked.

"She's just scared."

"Are you here alone?" Victoria asked.

Joan seemed to be intently listening. "Okay…. With your son."

"How did he die?" Victoria asks.

"Accident."

"Like a car accident? What kind of accident?"

"It was an accident…. You don't want me here? Okay." Joan moved away as Paul approached the northwest room. He looked to Victoria. "Go close. Get closer," he instructed.

"Okay, Angela, may I come close?" Victoria asked.

"Whatever we're doing, keep doing it. It's working," Paul said, heading off to the kitchen area.

"It's so cold! Do you feel it? I never get cold that much…." Joan started shivering.

"How old are you, Angela?"

No response.

"And your son, what is his name?"

Pausing to concentrate, Joan shook her head. "Nothing."

"Are you here with your son?"

"She says, 'I am dead.'"

"But is your son with you?" Victoria asked.

"She says … it was an accident. Okay!"

"Did she say what kind of accident?"

"He died in the room we were in. Downstairs we went … to the barn?"

"Okay."

"He died there."

"In the cellar of the barn?"

"Yeah."

"What happened?"

"His Dad … his Dad got mad."

"How old was your son?"

"He was young. Seventeen."

"And how did you die, Angela?"

"She lost a baby. That's why in that room I feel baby suffering."

James entered the northwest room. "Is it just me, or can you guys feel the energy slowly going everywhere now?"

Both Joan and Victoria answered his question with a yes.

"Oh God. There's a lady here. She, um … she's a mother of these children."

"Is there anything she needs from us?" Victoria asked.

"She says just … go."

"And what is she scared of?"

"Of Moses. Of men."

"Would she be more comfortable if I left the room?" James asked.

"I have to get out of this. She doesn't like you. Like in the kitchen."

"I can respect that. I'm sorry. So it seems she doesn't allow the flash to work? He also doesn't allow the flash to work. So is it because the flash hurts them? Bothers them? They find it intrusive?" James asked.

"Yeah. She says it's 'privacy.' It's privacy; I don't know."

"Ah, okay. I apologize for invading your privacy. Do you accept my apology?"

Joan stopped to listen, long pause, "Yes."

"I'm getting a heaviness in my chest."

"Well, thank you, Angela. I hope you find peace." Victoria said.

"Then get rid of the men. I don't know what men she's talking about. There are so many people that are here in this house. She doesn't like two men. It's a father-in-law or something and a husband?"

"Is there somewhere, Angela, where you can go to feel safe?" Victoria asked.

"Upstairs in the bathroom. She asks me to go upstairs. Will you go up with her?"

"Can I go up? Yeah," Victoria stated. Joan and Victoria headed to the master bedroom on the second floor.

[A female whisper is captured on the digital recorder: "April!" Indistinguishable words, then, "April!"]

I entered the northwest room and sat down. "Do you mind if I sit here with you? Is that you, Miriam? Miriam, is that you? Can you make that light go off? Please? If you make that light go off, I will leave this room."

Light stayed on.

"Can you do that, please?"

Light stayed on.

"Okay, I'll put this away. I'm going to turn it off. If you can make that light go off, I will leave this room."

Light stayed on.

"No? How about if I said 'please'?"

Light stayed on.

"Are you upset that we're here? Does our presence disturb you? How long have you lived here? It's a very nice room. Do you sit by the window? Are you upset that I'm here?"

No replies on the digital recorder.

"Who's the young man who stays here and helps you? He seems very polite?"

No reply.

"Thank you."

I headed out and met Paul, who was taking photos of the kitchen area. We headed to the master bedroom on the second floor.

James entered the room with Victoria and they experimented with the static detector.

Victoria tried to assure the spirit energy of their harmless intentions. "May James approach you?" she asked.

James approached the static detector and as he did so he spoke reassuringly. "It's okay, I'm not here to hurt you. You can trust me. I'll just move a little bit closer, okay? It's okay, you don't have to go away. You can trust me."

The light went out.

"Ah, you're still Miss Shy — I'll just back out. It's all right," James said, moving back to the doorway.

"Don't be afraid," Victoria said.

"You still here?" James asked.

James watched as Joan was in contact with Angela. He had heard that ghosts did not like the bright lights from the camera flash, and that they found it intrusive. He felt that the male spirit was present as well, and had theorized that the flash would not work any time the male was present. He took a picture and although the flash was charged and ready, it did not go off. He did this to confirm that the male spirit was there. Remembering what Joan had told him, he said aloud, "I forgot that you found the light intrusive." He then closed the flash and said he would leave it closed.

[Immediately James's digital recorder captures a male voice telling him to "Fuck off."]

"It's okay, I'm going to move further away. Maybe she left," Peter said.

"I still see a blue light," James said…. Then the light glowed bright again.

Peter came downstairs and retrieved his digital recorder and called out to me. I meet him at the bottom of the stairs.

"I didn't have a recorder with me when Joan picked up on Angela in the washroom. She [Angela] lost a baby at six months; a boy, miscarried because of the abuse and she" — indicating Joan — "saw blood all over the floor of the bathroom and then she left."

Paul and I headed upstairs to meet with Joan, James, and Victoria.

"You were talking about the husband; she didn't like it," Joan started.

"I asked what his name was but she wouldn't …" Peter stated.

"Where is it and where is the baby…? She said she never saw it; he just took it," Joan said.

"Buried in the floor in the barn. So I asked her if she would come out with us to the barn and point to where …" Peter said.

"She said, 'No.' She's scared to go. No way. You asked if we come is she going to help us, and she said, 'No.' He will kill you if you go out there. And she was saying he has tools," Joan explained.

"Yeah, how he was going to kill us?" I asked.

"Yes, tools, tools …" Joan said, seeming frustrated.

"So he's going to kill us if we go out there. Tonight?" Paul asked.

"She says if you go, because Peter was asking so many questions about the husband. She doesn't like it. She's scared."

"So it's possible somebody's buried under that hump. Maybe?" Paul said.

"Somewhere. It's a baby. It might be a six-month … fetus?" Joan stated. "This one, also. We don't have just one. We have … I told you, the guy was working on something in the barn. I don't know what. Now I can see baby, that one and some others, old … old men, old woman."

I felt an immediate and severe pain in my right leg that almost brought me to the floor and I steadied myself on the wall.

"What? Something kick ya?" Paul asked.

"No."

"Well what'd it feel like?" Paul asked.

"Like some kind of impact to my thigh, something ..."

"Is that normal?" Paul inquired.

"Is that normal?!" I said, starting to laugh.

"It's not normal, come on! He has pain," Joan said.

"Well, you know what? We're stirring them up, this is a good thing," Paul added.

"This is what Joan was is saying, apparently we're disturbing them and that something is going to happen if we stick around long enough," Peter explained.

"Oh yes, just get ready, okay?" Joan warned.

"Well that's the idea. What we're doing is going from room to room, everybody's talking to them at once and we're driving them crazy," Paul suggested.

"He's here, now," Joan reported.

Peter pointed to the E. Probe. "Can you touch that box? I just want him to touch that box to let us know that he's here. Are you afraid we'll find out about you and what kind of a man you are?"

No response.

"When Joan was sitting in there talking to Angela, all of a sudden I could feel a breeze like somebody was walking right through me," James reported to Paul.

I told Peter and Paul to suit up and the three of us would head out to the barn while the rest of the team remained in the cottage. They started to put on their winter jackets.

"He's coming with you, right now," Joan told us.

"That's fine. He's threatening to hurt us, so it's okay we might hurt him back," Paul said.

"Don't say that!" Joan said, laughing nervously.

We left Joan in the bedroom and decided to go the barn. As the three of us headed to the back door, Joan caught up to us.

"Where are you going?" she asked.

"Heading out to the barn," I told her.

"You shouldn't go out there, something is there," she said, trying to convince us to remain in the cottage.

"We have to go. You stay here with James and Victoria."

"Be careful out there!" she said.

Peter, Paul, and I left the cottage and moved out into the night, the icy snow crunched underfoot as we walked silently toward the barn. Everyone's thoughts were focused on what we might encounter there — it's not often we get threats from the dead. The temperature had dropped and it was very cold. The sky was clear; the moon hovered above full and bright casting long shadows from the surrounding trees out across the snow.

Back inside the cottage, James popped the bathroom door open to take a photo. After several seconds of the door being open, he could feel cold air go rushing by him, tugging at his body. He turned and headed upstairs to where Joan and Victoria were. James went to take a photo and again his flash would not work, so he stepped out into the hallway to test the flash and as soon as he left the room it worked.

"Nathan," Joan said.

"Who?" James asked.

"He is trouble," she stated.

Outside, we stopped at the barn door. Peter unhooked the chain latch, and from not far off came the eerie howl of a pack of coyotes. Paul looked around the side of the barn. "They sound close by," he said, shining his flashlight along the edge of the barn.

"Yeah, let's get inside," I said

I nodded to Paul, who pulled the door open wide and stepped back out of the way allowing me to fire a shot into the opening in the hopes of catching something unaware.

We stepped in and swung the door closed behind us. "Not any warmer in here," Peter observed, scanning the interior main level with his flashlight.

"Man, now I'm feeling dizzy!" Peter reported.

"You going to be alright?" I asked.

"Yeah."

"Let's go up," Paul said, climbing up onto the small deck to the ladder.

Peter followed him up into the loft. I remained on the main floor taking photos in the animal stall.

Peter started to explore the loft as Paul took random pictures.

"There is something up here!" Paul yelled down to me, and I quickly made my way over to the ladder.

"What the hell!" Paul called out. "It smells like shit!"

I had just arrived at the base of the ladder when a cold gust of air came down the ladder and hit me. It carried the stench of human excrement, forcing me to step backwards. The guys came down to the main floor. "Did you smell that? What was it?" Paul asked.

I paused a moment. Normally this sort of thing is associated with something evil. I looked at them and told them, "This is not a good sign; we need to be careful." It was at that moment that we remembered what Joan had told us prior to us heading out to the barn.

Paul moved to the stairs and, looking down, he said, "Let's check the cellar."

We all headed down into the cellar and fanned out.

"Anybody in here want to talk to us? You said you were going to hurt us if we come in here. Well, we're here!" He paused for a reaction. "Where's the baby? Where's the baby buried in here? Tell us! Knock on something!" Paul knocked on a wooden beam in an effort to provoke a response.

"Where's Angela's baby buried? We know he's here.... We know he died because you abused Angela," Peter said.

"Ask him if I'm standing on the grave," Paul said.

"Is this where the body is buried? Under Paul?" Peter yelled out.

"Is this where we need to dig? 'Cause we're going to dig!" Paul stated.

Peter checked his digital voice recorder for any hint of a response. Nothing was found.

After a few minutes we decided to head back to the cottage. Paul moved to the stairs with Peter a few feet behind him. I was still taking photos. Paul stopped at the bottom of the stairs and started to choke. Peter started to cough as well, although not as bad as Paul. Paul raised his camera and fired shots into the stairway, stepped back and fired again. Paul and Peter moved back into the cellar. "It felt like something was going into my throat, choking me," Paul explained.

"It was weird," Peter added.

Paul lifted his camera to review the photos. The first shot of the stairs showed a black and grey mist full of shadow and orbs. The next shot showed a normal, clear stairwell.

We climbed up out of the cellar. "It's better now — I don't feel like I'm choking! I don't know, I can't explain it," Paul said, standing near the door.

"Like a sandy kind of dust," Peter said.

"Yeah, kind of like a dust, or something like that. I've never felt that before," Paul reported.

"Let's head back," I advised, and the three of us exited the barn.

We had stopped outside the cottage to discuss what had happened and what it might mean, when we heard a strange clicking sound come from a large tree back at the barn.

"Did you hear that?" Paul asked. Peter and I both nodded and I moved off around the side of the van toward the old gnarled tree. Immediately the sounds stopped.

We checked the tree and found nothing except the feeling of being watched. As we stood there talking the clicking sound continued until Peter felt a sharp pain in his left chest, like being poked with a two pronged fork, then again the pain returned. While he rubbed the spot, describing the sensation to us, I thought of what Joan had told us: "He has tools." As we retreated back to the cottage the clicking sounds grew louder behind us.

In the cottage, Peter entered the studio and placed a pad of paper and a charcoal pencil on the table, with hopes that some spirit would be able to use them to communicate with us. James headed upstairs. He felt as he arrived on the second floor that there was a charged energy in the air and the scent of horses and freshly cured tobacco.

I headed straight for the second-floor master bedroom and stood in the middle of the room. James could sense someone moving toward him from the opposite corner of the doorway and it felt like the floorboards under the carpet were moving, as if someone were approaching.

James started moving down the hallway. Joan was downstairs and Victoria was now in the second-floor master bedroom. As James walked down the hallway he felt like someone was right behind him, observing him. He stopped to see if he could feel or hear anything and asked Victoria if she could.

"I don't feel anything, but my batteries just died," Victoria reported.

[James's digital voice recorder at that moment captures a male voice saying "Coffee."]

Peter entered the northwest room and approached the static detector, which was glowing once again.

"Angela, is this you? If it's you, turn the light off. No?" Peter extended his right arm across the small shelf unit the detector was standing on. "Can I shake your hand? Can you touch me, please?"

Paul took a picture of Peter from outside the room.

"Who was just talking there?" Paul asked.

"Who?" Peter asked.

"I just heard … a male," Paul reported.

The room goes silent.

"I just heard a male, talking!" Paul said.

"Okay, I'm waving my hand around the light here and it's not going out yet," Peter said, waving his hand.

"Stay there, Peter. I want to take a picture," Paul said.

"Hello, may I shake your hand? Hm, I'm feeling a tingling in my palm, but maybe it's because I have it outstretched. Hello? Okay now, the light's gone off; I touched the wire briefly, but it's only going off when I reach for the wire with my fingers," Peter said, retreating from the device. "Okay, sorry. I didn't mean to disturb you. I'm going to turn on the EM Pump again. The static light is just dim — very dim — and now it's brightening. That's it; can you make it brighter, please?" The EM Pump was a small battery generator which produced an electromagnetic field. The theory was that spirits could use this energy to manifest.

[The digital voice recorder captures strange electronic clicks on the microphone.]

Peter continued, "Just get closer to it; that's pretty neat, isn't it? Isn't that fascinating? Isn't that miraculous? Cheers! Here's to your good health, and mine," The light kept getting brighter.

Peter left the room and discovered a scraggly single line drawn downwards from the words he'd written on a small pad of paper, earlier. The charcoal pencil was missing, so he searched for it.

"No one has touched it," Victoria said.

Joan shared with Victoria that she'd like to talk to the owner about a particular painting she saw in the studio. "The pictures she's drawing are not … normal. She sees something and she draws whatever she sees. How many faces you see? She sees these people here in the house."

[The recorder inside the northwest room picks up a female's voice saying, "Oh, fuck!"]

"Alright guys, it's late, we need to wrap this up," I announced.

The team started to prepare to head home. Paul swept the main level. Peter entered the northwest room, shut the EM Pump off, and collected his equipment. He moved the recorder to the table next to the stairs.

I shut down the surveillance equipment and packed it away; Peter arrived and took one of the containers out to the vehicle.

We said goodbye and watched as Joan, Victoria, and James departed from the site.

"Okay, we'll let you know what's on the surveillance," Paul told Peter.

[Just then Peter's digital voice recorder captures two loud cracking sounds. They sound like two pieces of wood being banged together.]

As we locked up the house and moved out into the parking area, Peter said, "I thought I heard something, there." He mimicked the sound of small pebbles being thrown around the company van.

"I know, I sense we are being watched," I told Peter.

As we stood there talking, the feeling of being watch increased as did the sounds of clicking noises.

We said goodnight and headed home.

Conclusions:

- This investigation marked the first significant number of physical "warning signs" the team encountered together on the property.
- Joan picked up on the abusive relationship of husband to wife, similar to Joanna.
- Joan focused on the alcove under the staircase in the cottage. This would become significant later.
- Joan named the "Barn Boy" in the photo "Mark."
- Together with the results-filled pendulum session in the northwest room, and the female EVP, Joan concluded that woman had stood over Peter's left shoulder during the session.
- It was with much success that John Mullan's new static reacted in different ways to Joan and Peter.

- Joan picked up on a new name within the cottage, something we would need to verify, if possible.
- I received what I can only describe as impact pain in my right leg for the first time while in the barn cellar discussing a possible buried fetus.
- The first serious challenge was issued toward the barn cellar spirits by Paul and Peter. Paul had a coughing fit and Peter got a throat full of dryness, too. Paul captured a picture of mist at base of the cellar stairway.
- Paul and I reported smelling the stench of human feces originating from the barn loft.
- After Victoria, Joan, and James left for the night, Paul, Peter, and I talked outside and heard movement nearby but out of site and the sound of small objects (pebbles?) being thrown.
- Peter reported feeling a pair of double-pronged jabs over his heart. He recalled Joan's comments earlier in the evening regarding a male threatening to use tools to kill us if we proceed to dig in the barn cellar.
- Gunshot reports from the Spirit Box were recorded.

Side Note

Peter received a cautionary e-mail from Dawn Eglitis, one the team mediums, who had not been part of this investigation and had not attended the location. She had warned him and the team to beware of an angry man in his fifties, bearing a pitchfork. This communiqué was unprecedented at the time — and still is. Dawn does not habitually write concerning psychic warnings, and hasn't since.

6

FOURTH INVESTIGATION
FEBRUARY

We had set the arrival time for the rest of the team an hour later to give Peter, Paul, and I some time to spend with the owners of the property.

We met them in the kitchen and reviewed some of the information and evidence we had collected. Peter, as usual, placed his digital voice recorder on the counter while we spoke.

Peter mentioned the EVP we had captured of a female saying "Oui" during a Spirit Box session.

[Peter's digital voice recorder captures a faint female voice saying, "Hey."]

Paul and I stayed downstairs going through some of the photos we had captured with the female homeowner as Peter and the male homeowner headed upstairs.

He pointed out to Peter that the master bedroom's ensuite bathroom wasn't a washroom until about fifteen years ago and that there was a chimney on the south side of the building that had been taken down. He described burlap sacks used as insulation in the master bedroom on the second floor; they were along the northwest wall and were covered with wallpaper. He pointed out the northwest windows were not there originally and that he was the one who had added them. As he continued to describe the wallpaper-on-burlap sacks phenomenon, I heard a slight metallic key-rattling sound.

As they came back downstairs, the owner pointed out to Peter that the original washroom was where the current laundry room was on the main floor.

We all headed out to the barn for a tour and immediately went down into the cellar and huddled around the dirt mound.

"So would there be a problem if we did some digging down here?" Peter asked.

"No not at all, just be careful," the owner stated.

"We will. Just some small holes, and we'll fill them in. Just to see…." Paul added.

We came back up to the main stall of the barn, where the owners revealed it was used to pack asparagus, and then added that a previous owner stored gladiolas down there, too.

We left the barn and talked outside for a few minutes and then the owners wished us good luck and left the property.

A friend of Peter's who was interested in creating a video documentary of the team's investigations arrived. We all greeted him and Peter immediately took him on a tour of the property. Paul and I moved inside the cottage and found some old magazines in the living room, which the owner had found in the walls and ceiling of the home during renovations.

As I pick through them, I noted that they all seemed to have been published around 1905 to 1907 — it was quite a nice find.

Handing me one of the magazines, Paul pointed to photo of a building and commented, "It looks a bit like this house."

I studied the lines on the building, and while there were many similarities, it unfortunately wasn't the same house. Just then one of Paul's flashlights that stood on the table fell over, making a heavy bang. We both looked toward the table. No one had been moving at the time, nor were we near the table when it happened. A moment later there came a clicking sound from across the room. We shifted our gaze toward the northeast room and kitchen area. Immediately Paul and I moved toward the sound to investigate and the sound stopped. I entered the northeast room and he moved into the kitchen area but nothing was found.

As I walked around the space looking for some clue, I noticed that the room had no door, however the pins and hinges remained screwed to the door jamb. I walked over and pushed the hinge pin up through the guide and let it slide back down. I used my finger to bounce the pin up, allowing it to fall back again quickly. "That's the sound," Paul said, coming back around into the room.

We walked over to the table and examined the flashlight.

Paul stood it up and played with its centre of balance. "No way this thing just fell over by itself," he said.

"Well, they have our attention. Now what?" I said.

Paul and I set up the surveillance equipment and decided to have everyone leave the building for about an hour to see if in our absence we would capture any activity. The four of us left the site.

Second-storey audio/video surveillance:

There is heavy walking, the sound of work boots on hardwood flooring, even though the floors are covered with thick, plush carpet.

The room grows extremely bright without any evident cause and then becomes dark. Nearby there is a tapping sound as if someone were hitting a wooden object with a pencil.

The room goes very bright and then dark again. Seems like the camera iris is trying to focus on something.

There is a hollow bang of what sounds like two pieces of bamboo being hit together, something we have physically heard on this floor before. Then a male calls out, "Amy."

Side Note

Later, when this was reviewed, it made me think about very similar events we had recorded with other investigations. Whatever ghosts may be, they seem to have a solidness to them, not physically like you or I, but something of an energy that retains shape. They are invisible the majority of the time and yet they cast shadows. Their touch, although cold and electrical like static, is as real and is as solid as ours. They affect background lighting when they pass a video camera, as if the lens thinks it sees something, and they make sounds when they walk as if applying weight to the floor or stairs.

Main floor audio/video surveillance:

Older female says: "Get my pole."

Male replies but the words are undistinguishable.

All goes quiet.

We met up with Joanna and drove back to the property.

We entered the house and headed upstairs to conduct a Spirit Box session. We moved through the open area and entered the master bedroom.

Joanna, following Peter into the bathroom, claimed to have caught the shadow person walking in front of her. Peter reported that when he entered the room, he thought he detected the vague scent of male body odour, by the time he stopped walking and stood in the centre of the room. Joanna's theory was that Peter chased a person into the bathroom, which passed her. Peter reported the air seemed "thick" where he stopped.

I settled in and set up the Spirit Box. I connected the external speaker and turned it on, and set the system to sweep at 100 milliseconds through FM channels.

"Alexander?" Peter began.

Spirit Box — a male voice: "Talked to him before. Talk to him."

This first communication was extremely remarkable considering seven words came over white noise frequencies changing channels every quarter second on the SB-7 device.

"Is Emma here?" Joanna asked.

Spirit Box — a female voice: "Maybe."

"How long have you been here, Emma?" Joanna asked.

[EVP captured on digital recorder: "How many girls are there with you?"]

"Are you happy here?" Joanna asked.

Spirit Box — a female voice: "A lot"

Spirit Box — a female voice: "About eleven."

"Who do you hang around with, while you're here?" Joanna inquired.

Spirit Box — a young female voice "Minnie."

"How about Amy? Are you here, Amy?" Joanna.

Spirit Box: "Won't ... play."

"And how long have you been here?" Joanna said.

Spirit Box — a male voice, matter-of-factly: "One death. My daughter."

"I'm not hearing anything, are you?" Peter asked.

"I don't hear anything," Joanna stated.

Spirit Box — a female voice, almost singing: "Told ya so!"

Spirit Box — a male voice: "Enough! Can ya hug it?" Followed by wooden *clack* sound.

Spirit Box — a female voice: "Uh-huh."

Spirit Box — a male voice: "Seek ... me!"

"Is anyone here who wants to talk to us?" Joanna began again.

Spirit Box — male voice, mockingly: "Hear that? Ha ha!"

Joanna: "This is your chance!"

Spirit Box — a male voice: "I wanna."

Spirit Box — a female voice, surprised: "You what?!"

Spirit Box — a female voice: "If I were you, you'd come away."

"Well, we're going out to the barn!" Paul jumped in.

Spirit Box — a male voice, sounding startled: "No!"

"We're going to look for that body!" Paul said.

Joanna giggled.

Spirit Box — a male voice: "Woman, go away."

Spirit Box — a male voice: "Slut!"

"Is there a bad one in the barn?" Paul asked.

Spirit Box — a male voice: "Punk."

Spirit Box: "Uh huh!"

Spirit Box — a male voice: "A freak! Ha ha!"

Peter: "Can you say that again a little louder, please? Why shouldn't we go in the barn?"

Spirit Box — a female voice: "I'd run!"

"What will happen if we go to the barn?" Peter asked.

Spirit Box — a female voice: "I'd run!"

Spirit Box — a male voice: "Please don't go!"

Spirit Box — a female voice: "Hide!"

Spirit Box — a male voice: "Don't slip!"

Spirit Box — a male voice: "I won't."

"What?" Peter asked.

Spirit Box — a male voice: "Thank ..."

Spirit Box — a male voice grunts and gives a goofy laugh.

Peter started to say something, just as more voices began under his words.

Spirit Box — a male voice with a Scottish or British sounding accent: "Why don't you use the cover?"

Spirit Box — a male voice: "Henry?"

Spirit Box — a male voice: "Yeah, what?"

"What's in the barn? Is there someone there who will hurt us?" Peter asked.

Spirit Box — a male voice: "Anna! Anna! AHHH!"

Spirit Box — a male voice: "Heathcliff!"

Spirit Box — a male voice, yelling: "Fuck you!"

Spirit Box — a male voice: "Big man."

Spirit Box — a male voice: "Thank you!"

Spirit Box — a male voice: "Cuff him!"

Spirit Box — a male voice: "I will!"

Spirit Box — a male voice: "Trusty."

Spirit Box — a male voice with a Scottish or British sounding accent: "Hello!"

"Can you say that again, please?" Peter asked.

Spirit Box — a male voice: "No. Enough."

Spirit Box: There is the distinct sound of a gunshot.

Spirit Box — a male voice: "They're dead!"

Spirit Box — a male voice: Anna...? Where—?"

Spirit Box — a male voice: "Where are you?"

Spirit Box — a male voice: "Freak."

Spirit Box — a male voice: "There ya go."

Spirit Box — a female sneezes loudly.

Spirit Box — a male voice: "How soon?"

Spirit Box — a male voice: "The barn."

Spirit Box — a male voice: "Like leverage."

Spirit Box — a male voice: "Hear that?!"

Spirit Box — a male voice: "Dad ... here are ... you?"

Spirit Box: There are two more gunshots.

Spirit Box — a female voice: "Accident."

Peter began a pendulum session.

"Is someone hiding in the washroom, right now?"

Pendulum: yes.

"Can you make that bigger, please?" [Referring to the swing of the pendulum.]

"Are you a woman?"

Pendulum: growing yes.

"Are you the woman who's been abused? Beaten by her husband?"

Pendulum: bigger yes.

"Is your name Angela?"

Pendulum: bigger yes.

"Is your surname Davidson?"

Pendulum: yes, still growing.

"Your name is Angela Davidson?" Peter continued.

"Ask her if she knows he can't abuse her anymore," Joanna added.

"Do you know that, Angela?"

Pendulum: yes.

"He can't hurt her anymore," Joanna repeated.

"Does he try to hurt you, still?" Peter asked.

[An EVP of a whine is captured.].

"Is he afraid of us?" Peter asked.

Pendulum: yes.

"Is there something in the barn he doesn't want us to find out about?"

Pendulum: bigger yes.

[There is an EVP of a male grunting and then a cough.]

"Is something buried under the barn?" Peter continued.

Pendulum: large yes.

"Is he afraid we'll find it?"

Pendulum: large yes.

"Will he hurt us if he thinks we'll be getting too close to finding it?"

Pendulum: yes.

"Do a control question: Is it summertime right now?" Joanna suggested.

"Is it summertime right now?" Peter asked.

Pendulum: neutral swing.

"Is it summertime, now?"

Pendulum: no.

"Is it still Angela I'm speaking with?"

Pendulum: neutral swing.

"Am I speaking with somebody else?"

Pendulum: yes.

"Are you friendly?" Peter asked.

Pendulum: larger yes.

"Are you a woman? Will you come out to the barn with us?"

Pendulum: neutral swing.

"Will you come out to the barn with us?"

Pendulum: no.

"So you won't? Are you afraid?"

Pendulum: neutral swing.

"Are you afraid of what's out at the barn?"

Pendulum: yes.

Peter ended the session by saying, "Thank you and we intend to go out to the barn."

"Who killed the cat?" Paul yelled out, referring to the cat in the barn.

[An EVP captures a male yelling, "Sully."]

We moved to the main floor and prepared to head out to the barn.

[Upstairs the surveillance camera audio records a male yelling, "Get out."]

The team moved out and made their way to the barn, Peter pulled the door open and we entered. Once again, the coyotes were howling.

"That's creepy," Paul said as he stepped into the barn.

Peter followed Joanna into the storage area.

Paul and I headed up to the loft. I placed my digital recorder on a support beam and moved away to explore the loft. Paul walked to the far end and climbed a ladder to a door to outside, used for hay.

Peter and Joanna climbed up and joined us. Peter placed the recorder down on an overturned tub and faced it into the loft. He set the pistol and E. Probe in the straw, and placed the photo of Barn Boy in the centre of the barn.

I set up a pair of static field detectors near the hatch. Almost immediately they lit up.

"Oh, look," Paul called out, referring to the static detectors.

[Peter's digital voice recorder picks up a burst of static and a scraping sound.]

The scraping sound becomes louder. "Do you hear that?" Peter asked.

"Yeah. Down there," Paul replied.

"I just heard a thump. Did you hear that?" Peter said.

"It's down there! Come on up join us," Paul called out.

We watched as the static detectors glowed on and off for a few minutes.

"Let's go to the cellar," I said, heading to the hatch.

We had started to leave when Joanna passed the detectors and the diodes blinked off. She moved slightly away and they started to glow bright. She leaned over and passed her left hand over them, and only one went off. She pulled her hand back and it came on again. This time she passed her right hand over them and they both stay lit.

"What's the name of the guy in the picture, please? Can you shout it out?" Peter called out.

Paul took a photo, looked at it on-screen, then said, "They're here." A strange mist that we could not see with the naked eye was evident in the photo coming down from the ceiling of the barn from east to west over the pistol.

Paul reported his brand new camera batteries were dead.

I handed him new batteries.

We descended the loft ladder for a break.

[There is a sound of some loud shifting movement, like cloth rubbing, on the recorder.]

Paul commented again from below on the picture of mist he took in the loft.

[Another loud shift of cloth near the recorder, followed by a male chuckle.]

Paul, Peter, and Joanna moved into the cellar while I remained on the main floor.

There was more shuffling and wooden creaks in the "empty" loft as the team was downstairs. I knew no one was up there (well, at least no one that breathes). Then a heavy step was taken through straw.

The team came up to the ground floor.

Peter called up the ladder through the hatch, "Who's gun is that?"

[The digital recorder captures a male sniff.]

"Whose gun is that? I need a name!"

[There is clicking and shifting sounds near the recorder, as if someone's trying to stay still, waiting for the team to leave, but observing them from above. The an male voice saying "Shit!" under their breath as they're shifting. There is a tap near the recorder as Peter addresses him, saying, "You back up in the loft, buddy?" — he pauses — "You back in the house?" There is a shift and soft impact near the recorder and then another sound of shifting/ stepping in straw; a soft crunch, underfoot near the recorder.]

Peter remained on the loft ladder as the rest of the team moved out the barn door. Peter took a few more photos and then came down to join us.

[As we stood outside the digital recorder captures a male voice: "Take care of it." Then another soft straw-crunch.]

Inside the cottage the surveillance cameras is capturing activity:

[On the second floor, a male yells out, "Emma!"

On the main floor system, "Hey!" A Male voice.

Back upstairs, the banging of wood together.

A strange yellow glowing orb comes from the kitchen and enters the living room past the camera toward the front door. Following the orb is the sound of heavy walking through the main floor.]

We made our way back to the house.

[As we enter, the EVP records a male yelling, "Hey!"

A moment later a male says, "Miriam."]

As we moved into the studio room on the main floor the house went quiet.

We spent about a half hour moving about the house taking photos and then decided to call it a night.

Joanna and I remained in the house, packing up the equipment, while Peter and Paul headed back to the barn to retrieve the digital recorders and pistol.

Once everything was packed we all said our goodbyes and headed home.

Conclusions:

After a few months on the project it had become apparent the challenges we faced here were numerous:

· From the age of this property and the amount of spirits here it was becoming difficult to sort them out.

· Each visit seemed to bring varying results and dramatic changes in activity. Over the building's long history many people came and went, and this had not changed. Given the multitude of spirits, the house seemed almost like a drop-in clinic.

· I had to wonder about that EVP when the male was recorded saying, "Miriam, they're all alive." Was he shocked by our arrival and were they expecting visitors in the form of other spirits? This truly was starting to appear as a meeting place for the dead.

- After careful analysis of the information collected via our recording and mediums we identified five distinct eras existing on the grounds:
  - very early history — 1840s
  - late 1920s to early 1930s
  - 1940s
  - late 1960s
  - the present
- Our major hurdle was that the ghosts did not co-exist, meaning that the groups of spirits phased in and out with the eras. This made it difficult to prepare and ask questions, as it was impossible to know who or what may be there at any given time. It was only after the fact, upon analysis of our recordings, that we knew who was present at the time.
- The other major problem was, after the events in the barn with the stench of human excrement and the photo Paul captured in the loft, I was becoming concerned for our safety. In view of these events I became aware of the possibility that a malevolent entity could be lurking in the shadows, manipulating the other spirits ... and even the living.
- The fact that this was a church in the past where something bad had occurred, such as a murder, suicide, or abuse, meant a desecration of the property, which could attract dark entities. We needed to watch for other signs; we needed to be careful.

7

DIGGING DEEPER

The photo of the boy in the barn loft posed a deep mystery, so we tried everything that we could think of to find a rational explanation. First, I had Peter check with the camera manufacturer to explain other ways that this image could have appeared. Here is the exchange of correspondence between Peter and the camera manufacturer.

Product Group: Sony
O/S: Windows XP/XP MCE
Model: DSC-S730 12345349
Question: Is it at all possible that a Sony Cyber Shot purchased new in 2007-08 can capture an image that has been broadcast via satellite or via digital cable when it does not contain a receiver?

On November 3, 2012, a series of photos were taken of an abandoned barn loft and in between the "regular" images, a very clear face of a young male appeared. I would like a Sony technician's official written assessment of this phenomenon, please. Thank you.

To Peter
Thank you for contacting Sony Support.
I understand that the Camera recorded the face of a young male when

capturing the images of an abandoned barn loft. The Camera does not have the ability to capture an image that has been broadcast via satellite or via digital cable. Based on the information you've provided, it appears that the issue is due to a malfunction. I suggest that you initialize the Camera and check the operation. You can initialize the Camera using the "Initialize" option in the Setup1 menu.

Thank you for understanding.

Sony of Canada, Ltd.

To Sony

Thank you very much for your prompt reply to my query.

Noting this anomaly occurred over a month ago and that it hasn't happened since (nor during the four plus years of previous use prior to Nov. 8th, 2012), what should I be looking for when choosing the "Initialize" option?

Is there a digital record of malfunctions or problems stored within the memory of the camera that is accessible through this option that may be of help? (I can't pretend to know what all the technical capabilities of this product are, so I must ask.)

I could describe the sequence of images before, during and after the appearance of the anomalies in further detail, or I'd be happy to forward them to you for your own reference, if you wish.

Have you personally heard of a similar malfunction occurring in other (receiver-less) digital camera models in your experience as a technician? Does this happen in newer models that DO possess a WiFi component?

Again, thank you very much for your helpful reply, so far. Please let me know if you'd like me to forward the images-in-question.

Sincerely

Peter

To Peter

I understand that you wish to know the option to be selected while initializing the settings. Please select "Initialize All Settings" option while initializing the Camera. It will restore all the settings in your Camera to factory default settings.

Also, due to incorrect settings the issue may occur with all the Cameras.

However, if the issue persists, please contact our telephone support staff who will be happy to provide further diagnosis and assistance at: (877) 899-7669.

Thank you for understanding.

To Sony

Thank you for the explanation regarding what will happen when I select the "Initialize" function, but I feel like my larger questions are not being heeded.

You say, "due to incorrect settings the issue may occur with all the Cameras," but is it even FEASIBLE that an "incorrect setting" can result in an undeniably clear colour image of a young man's face taking up most of the frame, while part of the background of the environment the photo was taken within can also be recognized through or behind the image of the person?

If a phenomenon such as I describe is NOT technically feasible, using the Cybershot model I have described (keeping in mind this — or any other malfunction — has NEVER happened during the years before or during the month since this picture was taken), would Sony be prepared to accept the idea that one of its fine products may very well have captured visual proof of what is referred to as paranormal phenomena?

I hope that I'm making it clear that my line of questioning cannot simply be brushed off as just another customer's standard tech question.

I realize I'm asking the tech experts at Sony to tread into some potentially controversial waters here, however if it is NOT possible for a full-fledged image to appear as it did, then what alternate explanation can Sony offer, please?

I humbly request that this issue be reviewed amongst more than one tech support team member before I receive a reply. The offer to send the sequence of images taken including the "mystery pictures" still stands (please see below). I would appreciate it even more if I heard back directly from the Head of Tech Support, him/herself. (If this process will take longer to accommodate me than the standard twelve-hour reply window, I do not mind in the least.)

As always, thank you very much for your valuable time with my line of questioning.

Respectfully,

Peter Roe

To Peter

I do understand your concern regarding the possibility of paranormal phenomena that might have taken place on the image captured by the Sony Camera. Based on the information you have provided, I suggest that you capture some more images using the Camera and check whether these images too contain the young man's face like you have described, then there is a malfunction occurred in the Camera. If the newly captured images do not contain this type of appearance, then possibly the image that you have previously captured is due to the paranormal phenomena. Thank you for your time.

Sony of Canada, Ltd.

Side Note

It is interesting to note that many years ago Sony had a paranormal division that worked on special projects. They did away with this division and currently they seem less than eager to speak about this type of phenomena.

In the meanwhile, we sent a copy of the image to a few local business people within the community to see if anyone might recognize his face.

Peter received information that a long-time resident had seen the photo of the boy. The resident said that she had gone to school with the boy and that he had died in 1965 in an accident, and she wanted to know where we got the picture from. Peter confirmed the boy's name was Ricky and that he had died when he was only a young teenager after being hit by a truck while riding his bicycle.

This was extremely interesting, however we could not move forward with this information as I felt for integrity we would require multiple sources to confirm his identity. One eye witness to something that took place almost fifty years ago wasn't the best source of information; people make mistakes and become confused by similarities over time, it's only natural. The search continued.

8

INDEPENDENT MEDIUM TOUR #1
EARLY MARCH

Peter knew of a medium that came highly recommended, so he contacted Barbara Ford of Inspirit Centre in Georgetown. We felt it would be advantageous to have a specialist not attached to our team or the owners to tour the property and possibly provide new insights, or at least confirm some of the information we had already compiled — in a sense, to put fresh eyes on the subject. Barbara had no prior knowledge of the building, or its history.

Peter and Barbara entered the house and settled in the studio.

Barbara started to share her take on the house almost immediately. "So this place feels to me [like] it has a lot more stagnant energy; more cluttered energy that's not necessarily sentient of any nature. But what it feels like is that there used to be a family here, but really, really hard-working, like, really hard, physical manual labor, living here. So they've changed the layout of this house too, yes?"

"Yes. Well, the current owners to some degree, but the people before them, they did some changes, too," Peter answered.

"Is the second storey original? Do you know?" she asked.

"No. That wasn't there before."

"Okay. Was it mostly these two rooms? That's what it kind of feels like."

Peter and Barbara entered the northeast room.

"By 'stagnant,' does that mean many energies, sort of clustered, more than sort of a singular energy?" Peter asked.

"I think its stagnant energy kind of like your dustbunnies, like it just kind of pools and pools; it doesn't have any consciousness or anything to it. There's no flow through the house; it just builds and builds and builds. That's what it feels like is happening here. The current owners that are living here feel tormented, though. Have they ever expressed any?"

"Actually, no." Peter explained that the current owners didn't feel any negativity in the house and had actually had guests feeling so comfortable that they are reluctant to leave!

"Interesting, because I don't pick up that at all; I don't feel any warmth here. This place feels to me very cold, energetically, fairly negative. That's what I'm feeling like with the 'tormented'; it's like an internal thing."

"Could it be not these owners, but maybe previous owners?"

"It could be. The hard thing with this house is — 'cause I'm not seeing a ghost of any sort here — I'm just picking up on energy here and when it's such an old house, it's hard to say what time period that this happened in. But it feels fairly current. So if it's not these owners, it would be the ones right before that I'm feeling."

"Okay. It's a layer that's closer to us than way back when."

"Yeah, closer to the current time. When I stand at the front door, that's where I feel more of the original owners, where I see really hard ... physical ... labour. Like really hard manual labor; really hard-working people" — she paused — "Not ... affluent, but really hard-working."

After observing the quietness of the house and lack of traffic outside, Peter and Barbara climbed the stairs to the second storey. Upon reaching the top, Barbara paused.

"Yeah, a lot of stagnant energy."

"Still, huh? So it's safe to say it pervades the place?" Peter asked.

"Yeah, it's full."

They made their way into the master bedroom, where Barbara looked over the ensuite bathroom for a short period.

"Yeah, I don't see any spirits here. It does feel full, though, like as far as the energy goes."

"Huh, they must be on vacation. It's their day off."

She laughed. "Well, like I said before, they sometimes run from me, but I don't feel anything here."

"Nothing negative in particular with this larger room?"

"Yeah, the bathroom, I get the sense of … of illness. Like a debilitating — where it would get worse and worse and worse? That's what it feels — somebody with this and that energy, feels more male … here. But I don't see an actual spirit; nobody's actually popping through."

Barbara continued, "This is one of these spaces that are really hard to keep clean, energetically-speaking, because you've got really little windows, you've no natural flow of energy and you've got all these spots like …. this bathroom is problematic by its nature. There's no natural light and there's no flow of air. Like everything just sits and pools and pools and pools. So whatever happens in this space, stays in there. I don't know if this would work for your recorder or not, but I would be tempted to set it up in here and close that door so you're not necessarily getting street noise and see what you pick up. You might pick up something. Yeah, because that's definitely the fullest room that we've looked through, and that's your best chance of getting something."

"That bathroom's only fifteen years old. Do you find that doesn't matter?"

"No."

"I guess what I'm getting at is the old theory that spirits can only go where they knew; what they were familiar with in life, hence the idea that a spirit seen walking through a wall, that's where a door was and that's all they know. But in our experience they can expand. Once they see what we can do, they can expand their reality and enter a place that wasn't there before their time," Peter explained.

"Yeah, I think because sometimes spirits — they follow energy and entities definitely follow energy — and that has nothing to do with the space. So if I'm right and there was somebody there who was in a lot of physical pain, dealing with a debilitating illness, that's going to draw negative energies to it. So even if it's only a fifteen-year-old space, they're going to go in and because there's no light and no air circulation to speak of; they're just going to sit and they're just going to stay in that space. So maybe if he goes off and maybe he's still alive, the energies that he attracted will stay there. I think maybe Richard and I define energy somewhat differently. With the bathroom situation, I don't think of that as a ghost. I think of it as a sentient being, but not a deceased person that would go in that space. So as far as deceased people, I don't feel any, here."

They stopped to look into the small bedroom. "Now we have natural light, so it's a little more open," Peter says.

"Yeah. It's way cluttered in that closet, but then you're backing onto the bathroom, as well, so it could partially be that."

They turned back toward the staircase.

"The banister looks fairly old. I wouldn't want to date it, but it's certainly before we had standards on how high your banister has to be. I've seen this a lot in the . . . more like your nineteen . . . thirties, houses where you'd fall over it. It's interesting that overall — and this surprises me because I drive by this house and I've always been fascinated by it, always wanted to see inside — I always got the impression that I liked the energy from the outside, looking in, but now, inside, I don't feel that at all. It feels like a very unwelcoming space."

"I wonder if it might be us, then. Because we're here we're not welcome?" Peter asked.

"I'm pretty sure I'm not welcome." She paused. "And that's probably the difference that you feel. Because I do clearings, it could be whatever's here doesn't want me around, because they don't want that happening. I've had that happen a lot. When I get called for clearings, I show up and there's a negative entity . . . [it] hits me as I walk in the door because they don't want to leave."

"Have you ever been physically pushed or shoved or kicked?"

"Um-hmm."

"Scratched?"

"No."

"No scratches? Good, well, we haven't had that happen here."

They headed down to the main floor.

Barbara laughed. "No, I don't see anything that would push me here. I don't know . . . it's interesting."

Peter opened the triangular door to the staircase alcove to show Barbara.

"Ooooh ... yeah. And you have a basement or a crawlspace?" Barbara asked.

"They do have a bit of a crawlspace; it's right under this ..."

"You've got ... there's an entity in there, for sure. About the size of a boy, grey skin ... Not a boy."

Peter locked eyes with her.

"The size of a boy, but not a boy?" Peter inquired. "Okay ..."

"Yeah. And that's the thing that's giving off the vibe to me that I'm not welcome here."

"So, it's not human? Never human?"

"No. No. That's where it was coming from, for sure."

Peter closed the door.

"We don't have to go down into it, but I'll show you where it is; a trapdoor," Peter said as he pulled it open.

"Oh yeah!" — Barbara paused — "There's at least one other one down there," she said, looking down into the hole.

"Non-human?"

"Non-human. For sure, non-human. Same thing, about the size of a ten-year-old, who would come up to about here on you."

Peter noted the height would be between about four and four-and-a-half feet tall.

"Yeah. Grey with eyes that go between black and red. I wouldn't be surprised if anybody's seen those eyes around when they've been sleeping. I think it comes out to the rest of the space, otherwise. Yeah, not nice spirits for sure," she explained.

"So if we placed a camera system or something down there, or a recorder, we'd probably get something?" Peter asked.

[Peter's digital recorder captures a gagging voice that sounds like, "Yeah!" with a slight echo to it.]

"Yeah."

"I don't think we've done a great deal of investigating down there, so I suppose it's possible while we're doing our thing up here."

"Is this the kind of energy that would run from light, or shirk it, or just find a shadow or a corner?" Peter asked.

"It'll hide in the shadows, so less light would be better, but then you'd have to think about personal safety, as well. Yeah, that's the problem stuff for sure, down there."

Closing the trapdoor and re-setting the floorboard, Peter said, "Wow, okay, that's the first I've heard of — even a hint of — non-human origin entities, here. That's news to me."

"Yeah. It has a male-like feel to it, but I'm sure it's not human."

They returned to the studio. "Are you feeling anything physical when you feel something like that?" Peter asked.

"It makes me feel sick to my stomach when I look down there, and I'd say the same when I look down the venting here. That's why I was asking about a basement, 'cause I could feel it coming up from there, the same as I could feel it coming out from the closet. So I think there's at least two. I'm not feeling comfortable about going down in that basement, but there might be more."

"Are they aware of each other?"

"Yeah, they're the same thing, whatever they are."

[The digital recorder catches a male voice saying, "How?!"]

"I wonder how they were invited here, somehow. What could've happened that attracted them?" Peter inquired.

"My inclination is that really bad things are going on in the basement. I think that draws in the energy and then it stays, and makes it easy to stay and easy to grow, because there's no flow, there's no light, there's no air flow. But I've no idea when they would've come; it doesn't feel part of the original owners. It feels … more like the '70s sort of thing."

"The lady [the female homeowner] … does she ever talk about the feeling of being watched?"

"No."

Barbara was completely surprised. "Really?"

"No. What she has shared with me is that she sees things, but she attributes that to the fact that she is an artist. Like, she'll see faces in tree bark and natural stuff. We found this painting really interesting." Peter shows Barbara the small painting containing several small faces scattered over the surface. "One of our mediums has commented that this isn't normal."

"It's not. So what did the lady say to the medium? What was her inspiration for this?"

"They didn't meet, but I think the owner said that painting was started after her mother died, so she was in an emotional headspace. She was seeing faces using her imagination or subconscious.…"

"That would be my concern; if she started that when she was here, that would be a big concern for me — that they're getting inside her head."

They moved into the kitchen and Peter described a recording he captured of sounds like someone was playing bongos using the sink. He thought it was a spirit. He finished by adding he wasn't afraid or startled by the incident.

"And that's the thing with entities like what I suspect are in the basement — what they feed off of is scaring people. When you get scared, you burst out energy and they feed off that and they get stronger and then it perpetuates itself. And that would be easy from the basement for them to come up for that sink noise-making, like through the flooring. Then the other thing would be is that it could be a water pipe, but it would probably be very hard to tell that."

"We haven't heard it since then. It was just that one afternoon when our recorders and surveillance cameras picked up this bongo-like playing."

Pulling out the asparagus knife that the owner left, Peter handed it to Barbara to try to read.

"I don't know how adept you are at psychometry?"

"Not so great, but I can try. I'm going to take these off, actually." Barbara handed Peter her hand and arm jewellery to hold while she read the knife. "I get a negative feel to it, but I can't ... get any details off of who held it or what they did with it, or anything. Sorry about that. I'm not so good with psychometry."

As Peter prepared to lock the back door behind them, Barbara commented on the house, one last time: "It's an odd space. It's interesting because it feels so nice, like when you drive by, it looks so warm and cozy. It doesn't feel like that inside, to me. Interesting."

Peter and Barbara went outside. Peter revealed the origins of the house as they walked around the exterior and then proceeded to the barn.

Inside the barn, Peter showed Barbara the asparagus knife sheath on the south wall of the stable area. She inspected the stable and asked after the whereabouts of the animal entrance through the wall.

Barbara started sharing her feelings of the barn: "So again, there's a fair amount of stagnant energy here, but it doesn't feel negative at all, to me." They moved out of the stable area and past the cellar. "It feels quite nice, actually, oddly enough. Basement?"

"Yeah, there's a mummified cat down there."

They entered the storage area between the stable and working garage.

"So this part is newer. Looks like renos have been done to it."

Peter pointed out the foot-long distance between the original barn and modern-day workshop.

"And he uses this space, periodically?" Barbara asked.

"Uh, yeah."

"Oh, I would expect you to pick up stuff here."

"How come?"

"It feels like being watched again, from out this way." She indicated the east wall, toward the road. "But outside the barn, watching in. I feel like, an older man with a white beard, hat ... farm-type clothes ..."

"Like overalls."

"Yeah, I see the suspenders, but I'm not sure if it's actually overalls or just pant suspenders, but it's probably more overall — I can see the shoulder straps."

"Older?" Peter asked.

"Yeah, yeah. Older, white hair, watching. Stronger energy but not negative. It feels like he's just observing, like, "What are you doing here?" kind of watching, but just past that wall. I would expect you could get him to talk on your recorder."

"If I ask him his name, now?"

"Uhh. We could try it, but I feel it is more likely if you set up your [equipment] and leave, then you'll get some talking."

"Okay, I see. They will converse. But he's the only one so far that —"

"Oh, you have got him on —"

"No, no, I'm asking you. He's the only one you pick up on so far in this general area?"

"Yeah. Um ... It felt like a child, but then it disappeared. So I'm not really sure if that was just somebody driving by, or if that's legitimate to this space. Yeah, 'cause it was here when we walked into the room and now it's gone. I feel the animals over there, but I don't feel them here."

There was an unidentifiable crunch or cough that sounded like it came from the direction of the east wall.

"What's that? Is that traffic?" Peter asked.

"I almost thought I could hear, like, a dog barking."

"Yeah, that's what I heard. It was like, *rowr, rowr!*" It was almost mechanical-sounding."

"There." The sound repeated.

"Unless it's footsteps in the snow. A crunch?"

"I don't know what that is."

"Sounds like snow crunching, to me," Peter said.

"Oh yeah? Maybe we have company."

"Hello? Sir, will you step closer, please? Let us know who you are?" Peter asked.

"There's someone else. There's a younger man … on this side." Barbara indicated the west wall.

"Outside?" Peter asked.

"Hm-hmm. White skin, dark hair; he's in farm clothing as well and fairly dirty. I expect he's the one that works with the animals a fair amount. It feels like the road didn't used to be this close to the barn. Would you be able to know if that's true?"

"It probably wasn't."

"It feels like the traffic is bothering him." She indicated toward the older man on the east side.

"Well, there used to be a railway line I think crossed here at one point."

"It feels like it wasn't this close, 'cause what I'm picking up from him — the man that's out this way — is that the traffic bothers him because it spooks the animals, he says."

"Makes sense. Do you get any negative vibes from either of them?"

"The younger male, he's more aggressive."

"How old would you say when you say 'young'?"

"I would say probably mid-twenties to mid-thirties, in that range. The older man I would peg more in his sixties. But they don't feel cognizant of each other, right now."

"Wow, 'cause I feel like we're surrounded!" Peter stated.

"No, but I don't feel that they're picking up on each other. I think we got one out here and we got one there; we're being watched from both directions. And I think you have more of that other stuff in that basement."

"What, you mean the negative …?"

"The grey things."

"Ah, so you're not comfortable going down there at all?" Peter asked, indicating the cellar.

"No. There's between one and three in there."

"There's a mound down there that's human-sized that we've been given permission to dig under just in case there's something there, because we're really curious about it."

"Have you looked at the mound? Do you pick up anything off of it?"

"Um … like, with meters and things? Tech?" Peter asked.

"Yeah."

"No, not really, no."

"Any of your mediums sense anything near it yet?"

"No. Even the owners are not quite sure what's in there."

After establishing that she wasn't dressed appropriately for a visit to the barn loft, Barbara shared more about the cellar.

"I don't feel human remains down there, but I do feel bones. But they feel like animal bones to me."

Without an explanation of its origin, Peter showed Barbara the blown-up photo of Barn Boy in the ground floor storage area to get her impressions of it.

"Yeah, there's something else in the photo."

"Okay. We think we see a face here, like a bulbous nose and a lip. It's like a low-angle shot looking up."

"But I feel something here, too. So when was this taken?"

"In November, in the loft, when Paul was alone. This person actually came up to his camera."

"Wow. Wooow! You know what you can do? You can shrink the picture down more and look right at this shadow and see how it changes. I think you'll get more details that way."

"You mean this shadow, or the lighter one?"

"Both. But I feel stronger on the dark, so look at that line and see what happens to it when you shrink it. Right in here, too, this whole section. I think you're going to see another face when you shrink it down and look at it."

Peter explained the short version of the Barn Boy story.

"Well, the hair and the glasses look more 1960s to me. The eyes are concerning. It looks like a very negative emotion is coming through, to me, in the eyes. It has a 'Who are you and what are you doing here; get out of my face' kind of look to it, but it looks like there's something that he hides. Have you found any odd things upstairs? 'Cause it feels to me — I suspect he probably lived here and hid things up there that he wouldn't want parents to see."

"No, we haven't found anything up there."

Barbara and Peter headed back outside; Peter closed the barn door.

"We've found more negative evidence come out of this place than the house, so it's kind of interesting, what you're picking up."

"Well, it's interesting, the spirits that were watching weren't upset with my presence, like they were in the house. Those entities didn't want me to be there, at the house. And I think they were picking up that what I do is remove things like them."

Peter and Barbara walked around the barn toward the road/east side to look for fresh footprints in the snow. They found nothing, so they went to the car.

"You know the green background color under Barn Boy's right ear? I see that a lot, with how I see, because of the energy that's coming off the spirit. Did you pick up any talking up there?"

"Not up there, no. In the basement, yes."

The walk-through completed, they left the site.

Conclusions:

- We became aware of two non-human, grey-skinned, boy-sized entities inhabiting the staircase alcove and crawlspace of the cottage.
- In the barn there was more stagnant energy, but then Peter and Barbara were watched by two ghosts from two separate eras from opposite sides of the building which were seemingly unaware of one another.
- Allegedly one-to-three more grey-skinned, non-human entities were detected in barn cellar, from the ground level.

Paul's photo of "Barn Boy"

Paul's photo of the face on the door, notice the heavy plasma-like mist

Peter's photo of the entity above the pistol, which only exists in the violet spectrum of light

Paul's photo of the group, notice the strange entities around Victoria, Peter, and James. Behind Victoria is a pronounced figure of a boy.

Mysterious mist in the loft

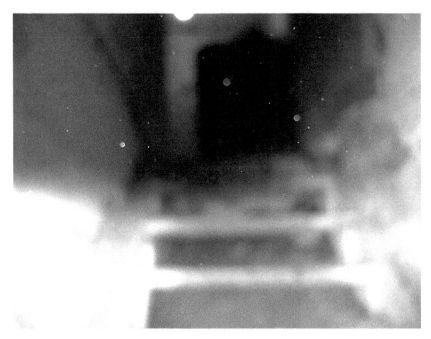

Paul took this photo as he began to choke

Paul's second shot of the stairway, now clear

Paul captured this photo of Peter in the mist; there are many faces around him

The British Bull Dog pistol found on the property — 32 caliber

The Searcher Group, (top-bottom) Paul Palmisano, James McCulloch, Victoria Jamie, Richard Palmisano, and Peter Roe.

INDEPENDENT MEDIUM TOUR #2
MID MARCH

The property owners wanted to bring in a team of mediums to tour the property, and Peter quickly volunteered to attend.

Peter arrived and brought the owners up to date on our progress and met with mediums Bonnie and Carol. He asked that the mediums share names, years, and eras that they picked up on as they toured the cottage and the barn. As Peter finished speaking of the barn, he observed Carol's gaze drop.

"You look like you've got something, already!" Peter said.

"I was getting stuff before I came. I was getting stuff about a young man. He's dead. I got he was strangled; I could just feel myself being strangled," Carol explained.

"I shared your photo of the boy in the barn with them," the property owner admitted.

"I asked Bonnie, 'Is there somebody buried on the property?' 'Cause it feels like somebody is buried on this property. And I watched ... I keep getting there's some water issues," Carol said.

"Well, the well's no good. But as far as water issues, this property is all very, very wet at times; we have a very high water table," the property owner explained.

"I remember the asparagus bed."

"I can move water, so ..." Carol added.

"I know you can move water and this whole area. Mind you, there is a lot going on in town and it's a very active area for ghosts, I believe, because of this water thing," the property owner stated.

"I feel this property has a lot of energy lines that may be attractive to spirits," Carol said.

The property owner left the house to retrieve blueprints of the property to use later for a preliminary dowsing (an ancient technique used to find things such as water and gold, mediums can use dowsing to find spirits and buried bodies. It is applied by using either a pendulum or two L shaped rods that when held one in each hand can swivel to point out areas of interest).

Having prepared her dowsing rods, Carol stood inside the kitchen doorway facing the studio.

"This part of the building, this is newer, right? The energy just shifts as soon as I move into there," Carol said.

Carol explained that her dowsing rods were swaying side-to-side, as if scanning. "So it's just searching, right now."

"Have you asked a question, mentally?" Peter asked.

"Yep. My question was, 'Is there a spirit in this house?' In the older part," Carol explained.

Carol was guided toward the northeast room; Peter and Bonnie followed. "This was a dining room at one time," Carol said.

"Usually they were bedrooms in the old days; split rooms. Split bedrooms. But who knows? This is a very old design," Bonnie added.

Carol moved inside the dining room. "There's a spirit attached, in here. There's some kind of a spirit in here. Somebody had a lot of problems breathing. I just want to keep ..." She inhaled then exhaled deeply. "It's a man. Sorry, I'm asking for the generation. So I'm up to the third generation in here."

"The third occupants, really?" the property owner asked.

"Yes, the third occupants, whoever the third occupants were. Do you know who they were?"

"We have a lot of history to look into!" Peter stated.

"Okay, so it's about the third occupants — coming from the beginning of the building. So I'm just asking if this is a man. Yes. Just asking, 'Are you a young man?'" She nodded yes.

Long pause as Carol re-set her dowsing rods and whispered under her breath. "Okay," she addressed the room, "I'm asking, 'Did you die of an injury?' That's what it feels like. Yes. So it feels like he died from an injury of some kind. In my mind I'm seeing like a fall, or something. Okay, he may have fallen off a horse...."

"Okay. So here, on the property, perhaps?" Peter inquired.

"Yeah, it was on the property. It feels like he injured himself across the back, right here. So he may have damaged his spine."

"All right, okay," Peter said.

"He feels very upset about it, like it was a stupid accident."

"I'm sorry, did he establish his age? Young or old, or ..."

"Young. Younger. Not a child, but younger ... I'm feeling like it's, uh ... mid-twenties?" Carol stated.

From the studio area behind Peter, Bonnie added, "Twenty-seven."

"Twenty-seven? Okay. I get the feeling ... the reason I asked if this was a dining room is because sometimes they would move the dining room furniture out and use the dining room as a state room, I believe. I just get the feeling this was used as a state room when he died," Carol said.

"You mean, like a sitting room? Or where they showed his body?" Bonnie asked.

"Where they showed his body."

"For a wake?" Peter asked for clarity.

"For a wake, yeah. It felt like his was in this room. That's what it felt like."

"Do you feel that he's here with us, or are you just picking up an energy?" Peter asked.

"Not sure if it's a vibration or not. You know, you can have them both."

Bonnie looked past the room out the window on the other side. "Would've been a much different view."

"He's still here," Carol said, lowering the rods and then holding her palm outward, feeling about from side-to-side. "Terrified; I've been hit before!" She laughs. "Yeah, they whacked me." Carol looked toward Bonnie. "Is there a portal in this room?" Long pause. "So I'm not good at names, but I'm asking for a name so in my mind I'm hearing 'John.'"

"John who?" Peter asked.

"Oh, you're asking the spirit that question?" Carol asked.

"I'm asking the spirit, yeah, to not give us somebody else's name to cover his, or whether it could very well be John," Peter stated.

"He's really upset that you're asking that question," Carol said, chuckling.

"I'm sorry, I need to know."

"No, no. No. No. He's just saying, 'You think I'd lie?' basically."

"I'm sorry, John, but I don't know you very well, so I'm just being introduced to you and I mean no disrespect," Peter said to the room.

"Okay, he says I have to explain my understanding of spirit from the other side. And for me, 'As in Life, So in Spirit,' which means if they were honourable in this lifetime, they were probably honourable in the afterlife. And he feels he was an honorable person, so ..." Carol explained.

"Okay, I appreciate that, John. Thank you."

"Sorry, I've never worked with somebody else doing this!"

"He's okay. John's okay." Bonnie said reassuringly.

"John, may I trouble you for your surname, please?" Peter asked.

"I was getting two different names and I'll have to give you what those were. The first one sounded like 'Scabatti' or something like that and the other one is 'Miller.' So, two different names."

"Okay. Just to be fair, my name's Peter Roe. I'm pleased to meet you."

"I also got the name, 'Burnside.'" Bonnie added.

"Like I said, names are not my strong suit."

"No, I got 'Burnside' loud and clear."

"It's not a very common thing for a psychic to achieve in our experience."

"I'm getting 'Burnside,' very clear. Maybe he was married to a Burnside, I don't know."

"Were you married, John?"

"I think it was more 'engaged.' He was engaged to a young woman. She's still alive?" Carol said, resetting her dowsing rods.

"Ask about his nickname for her." Bonnie suggested.

"Nickname?" Carol inquired.

"Yeah, his nickname for her. See if you get it." Bonnie repeated.

"Else?"

"'My Lola.' Just, 'My Lola,' and very possessive: 'My Lola.'"

"Okay, I'm not getting that."

"I don't know what that is, but that's what I got. Thank you! And he liked emeralds."

"John, what year is it, please?" Peter asked.

"It's about 1930s … -ish," Carol said.

"1932 in there, somewhere…." Bonnie added quietly.

"Sorry?"

"1930s."

"1930, 1932, in there."

"Early thirties, but it's not clear? Thank you."

"See, he just said — I don't know why he said that. He just said, 'Coming of age was very difficult back then.' And I guess stuff would've been around the First World War, wouldn't it?" Carol said.

"First World War and then …" Bonnie added.

"Depression?" Peter asked.

"Depression, yeah. He says it was just a very difficult time to grow up."

"Why would he show me an emerald ring?" Bonnie asked.

"I'm thinking green …" Peter said.

"Left hand; emerald ring," Bonnie stated.

"Birthstone? What month? Is there a …?" Peter asked.

"That's May. May, yeah."

"John, would you mind telling us if there are any other spirits here in the house with us, please?" Peter asked.

"What I hear is, 'One came back.' I believe it was the original builder, because he was watching things change. And he got upset. That's usually when they [spirits] start doing nasty hauntings, just to scare people, 'cause they don't want you to make changes. I've seen that happen. But he comes and goes, this particular person. I don't even get his name. Do you get a name?" Carol said.

"I just got — I think it's a woman … the name I told you?" Bonnie said.

"Yeah. Ella — no."

"Lola," Peter said.

"Lola. And the last name — I don't know if it's hers — but there's a 'Burnside.'" Bonnie stated.

"And I also … I was standing there and I was getting an 'Eloise.' Do we have an 'Eloise'?"

"No, not yet. We've picked up many names, through our equipment," Peter explained.

"Mmm. There are a lot of people here."

"Have you gotten any voice?"

"Hm-hmm. Oh yes."

"Good!"

"I feel like he died from a fall," Carol said.

"Inside the house? John? Or out?" Peter asked.

"He's out," Carol replied.

"On the property," Bonnie added.

"It was almost as if he was on a horse or a tractor, or something like that. That's what it felt like he died from."

"There's a tree involved, too," Bonnie said.

"Did you fall from a tree, John? Were you climbing a tree and …" Peter said aloud.

"I'll let you do that one, 'cause you're the one getting the tree," Carol said.

"Or did you fall and hit the tree as you were falling?" Peter asked.

"That's my guess. I think that's what happened. Hit the head …" Carol said.

"Hit his head, definitely," said Bonnie.

"So are you getting a horse or a vehicle?" Carol asked.

"Horse. But I don't know why I'm getting a horse," Bonnie stated.

"Well, that's what I got; a horse," said Carol.

"Yeah, this side of his head, right here," Bonnie said as she placed her palm over the right side of her head.

"Right side?" Peter confirmed.

"And going toward the temple."

"Sorry to hear that, John." Peter said, out toward the room.

"He was mad," Bonnie said.

"'What a waste,' is what I hear! 'What a waste! What a waste!' Now, okay, is there anything else you want to ask John before we move?" Carol asked.

"No, not at all. Thank you, John."

"Thanks, John!" Carol extended her arm toward the wall dividing the northeast room and the northwest room. "That's where the portal is."

"Portal's right there, yeah," Bonnie said.

"I know I'm thinking in terms of three-dimensional space, but is it vertically in the wall or is it like a column that goes …" Peter inquired.

"No, when I see them, if I turn my head quick, I can see it. It looks like a small tornado — that's about the easiest way for me to describe it. It whirls. Like, generally, he went out that one. I don't know if he came back in that one. This is what the spirit showed me. You have an in-bound and an out-bound," Carol said.

"Oh, is that right? Okay," Peter replied.

"Yeah. So, that must be an out-bound vortex."

"Do you find that anyone can utilize those vortices or they mainly energies or spirits that have something to do with the area?" Peter asked.

"When I've run into it, it's spirit, pretty well."

"It's peoples' spirits who will use them."

"I want you to check that corner. I've done it twice," Bonnie said, moving into the studio.

Carol moved to the corner. "I get a lot of tears. A lot of sadness."

Bonnie crossed the room and stood even farther away. "Yeah. I can get this far and then I start shivering."

"It's hitting my heart. 'My baby.' Somebody's baby died. It's a woman. I was just seeing her cradling the baby; she's holding the baby as it's dying. Oh, I have to move out of that," Carol said as she retreated away from the corner.

"Yeah. I could get this far and then the whole front of me is ice-cold," Bonnie signaled to Peter to come over. "Can you feel this?"

Peter moved closer to the corner space slowly.

"And stop every once in a while, just to feel it."

Peter advanced closer to the corner.

"It's right about there. It's like there was a big chair; a rocking chair or something there."

"Mmm." Peter scanned the area with his hand.

"Can't feel it?" Carol inquired.

"I'm feeling a draft, but because the eastern window is not insulated,"

"Okay, so ask to feel the emotion," said Carol.

"Of sadness?"

"Sadness. Profound sadness. If you're a woman, this is what you feel when your child dies."

"Well, I'm a dad myself, so ..."

"Okay, okay, so think how you would feel. That's the feeling you're going to have."

"This is a young child," Bonnie said.

"It looks like a babe-in-arms," said Carol.

"Could it have been stillborn?" Peter asked.

Bonnie paused for a moment. "No."

"So carried to term, and ..."

"I've got it at three months. Two to three months is what I got. And it died very suddenly," Bonnie said.

"It could almost be like Sudden Infant Death Syndrome? That's what it feels like," Carol said.

"Yeah, yeah, yeah. SIDS, yeah," Bonnie said.

"Does she share a name at all, or an era?" Peter asked.

"Mm ... I get 'Elsbeth' for the child," Bonnie said.

"I don't think that's what I was getting, though," Carol said.

"'Little Bess.'"

"Okay, maybe, sometimes it's really hard to hear them. Or things get garbled."

"No, I can't get her to talk. She's sobbing," Bonnie said.

"Yeah. Okay."

"Sorry, you said, Elsbeth?" Peter asked.

"Elsbeth, yeah. And she calls her Little Bess," said Bonnie.

"I'm sorry for your loss, ma'am. Is she able to hear us, you think?" Peter asked.

"She's crying so hard; I can't get her to talk to me. She's just looking at her ..." Bonnie said.

"She's totally ... in her grief; she's just totally there. I'd like your permission to get her out of here, to send her to the light where she can go back into peace. That's a long time." Carol asked.

"Should you try for the baby, too?"

"Yeah, she'll take the baby with her. She's such a young woman. I want to get more from her, first."

"She's eighteen. I get that she's eighteen and the baby's between two and three months," Bonnie stated.

"I've got one question I can't figure it out. Maybe you can help me. She's either committed suicide or this is just an energetic impression," Carol said to Bonnie.

"I've got the energetic impression. She's sitting in a chair almost like a nursing rocker."

"Do you hear squeaks here or squeaks in this room? An old rocker going back and forth or the floorboards are too loose?" Carol asked the property owner.

She shook her head no.

"So you've never heard that? Okay, so it's definitely energetic impression."

"She's showing us a particularly strong memory?"

"Yeah. Unfortunately you get a lot of impressions from older furniture and people in older houses. Sometimes they get very active; they get very repetitive, physically."

"She feels … bound," Bonnie said, locking her arms in a tight embrace.

"It's like when you've held something too long and you can't move anymore."

"Yeah, that's what I'm getting. And I'm trying to decide if she's moving the chair or the chair's moving, because she's just rocking in grief. It's like if you tried to get the baby away from her, you couldn't. She's —"

"Locked," Peter said, finishing Bonnie's sentence.

"Locked, yeah, that's a good way to put it. It's like her spine and shoulder's turned to steel; they're just rigid."

Bonnie and Carol quietly meditated, directing their focus toward the northeast corner.

"Ever sit in this area to paint? Do you ever get … sometimes feel sad? Just wondering if you pick up the emotions, or not," Carol asked the property owner.

"I … I am sad, sometimes …"

"Well, you'll notice it more right in this area."

"No. Frustration sometimes there, but not necessarily sadness," the owner said.

"You'll notice when you're painting over here, you're more energetic than you are anywhere else."

"Yeah, that's why I paint here."

"My feet are warm. My feet are getting warm, now," Bonnie said.

"I can start to breathe again; I don't feel so tight." Carol said.

"Did you get a date on her?" asked Peter.

"I'm trying to get her — I know she's eighteen, but she's not telling me the year. She just —"

"Or a surname or a first name?" Peter asked.

"No."

"The baby. Follow up on the baby."

"Elsbeth, a derivative of Elizabeth," Peter added.

"Yeah, which is probably why Little Bess."

"Maybe her name was Bess?"

"Maybe ..."

"Like a 'junior.' Or her mother. Or somebody that she knows," Peter said.

"Her impression's clear."

"See the vortex of grief that she descended into? Down, down, down, down.... Did you see it?" Bonnie asked Carol.

"No."

"No? Okay. It's red. It just goes down, down, down, down, down.... I think it just sucked the life out of her."

"Well, that's probably what depression looks like."

Peter directed the mediums to try and read the northwest room.

Carol spoke first: "This was a bedroom at one time. I see an old woman sitting on a bed. Like, an iron bed. She feels very weary."

"Does she show you where it — the bed — would've been placed?" Peter asked.

Bonnie moved, gesturing toward the west wall. "So she could look out the window."

"I think she's saying she's tired ... tired of living. I think she had a hard life and she's tired of living. She feels like a woman who was ... she didn't have a lot of expectations around life. I want to start crying. But it just wasn't like the way she expected and so there's a lot of sadness about this life that didn't really ... I don't want to say, meet her expectations ... but she thought it might've been a bit more than what it was."

"It was very meager. That's the word: meager," Bonnie explained.

"I just felt she was ... disappointed."

"She had very little in the way of belongings. That's not what she's talking about."

"It's emotional ... like, starvation. But not food. Emotional. And I get a sense that she was the mother of somebody who had this house. And they brought her here, but ... she had limited ... purpose. That make sense? Limited purpose?" Carol said.

"Were there lilac bushes here?" Bonnie asked the owner.

"There still are."

"Okay."

"Those suckers will keep going forever."

"Is she showing you?" Peter asked.

"Yeah, she is. She liked the cold."

"She liked the smell. She liked the cold."

"Is she sitting on her bed now? Watching us?" Peter inquired.

"Uh-huh. She does this with her hands" — Bonnie rubbed her fingertips together — "It's like a nervous habit."

"I get the sense that this impression that we're picking up of her was about the same time as she died. That's what it feels like to me. I'm just trying to decide what the thought was in her mind, because that's where I work with a lot of people on the Other Side; the thought that was on their mind at the time of death."

Peter observed Bonnie swaying back and forth on her feet. "Is she swaying like you are, Bonnie?"

"She's talking to me, right now. She's just saying — in a modern parlance — 'I'm done; I just want it over. I want ... gone.' That's in modern parlance. I'm just trying to get to how she would normally speak, because it's a different cadence. It's basically, 'Lord, I'm tired. Let it be over.'"

"Speaking in an accent? When you say 'cadence'?" Peter asked.

"Uh, more of a lilt. It's quite musical. I should ask her what she is."

"I see a very petite woman, very tiny, very petite."

"She likes linen; very fine linen like ... an embroidery, but it's a raised embroidery ... in the front. And she's got very thin, long hands and very bony — like, she's basically wasted [away]."

"She's living here alone? Unassisted?" Peter asked.

"No, but she's isolated in the fact that this is her room."

"They brought her here basically to wait for her to die."

"Bed's over there and there was a quilt on the bed and it's got navy blue in it. I think its wool, like a — what do they call those quilts; they make them out of everything?"

"Patchwork."

"Patchwork! That's it. The room's pristine, but it's very sparse."

"Yeah, it's like there's not a lot of furniture in here. There's a dresser over this way."

"Tiny little night table."

"Does she require anything to move around? Like a walker, or ..." Peter asked.

"She doesn't want to move. She doesn't want to move at all. She just wants it done."

"It's interesting while you're talking to her, before you started talking about that, what I was getting was, 'One life to live, thank God.' So basically, she's not expecting to incarnate some other time, but she's not thinking about crossing. She's kind of locked in that moment before she dies in her sleep. I got she's gone in her sleep, but she's sitting on the bed. So we're seeing her just before she lies down to go. And she's expecting not to go anywhere else; she's expecting that this is it."

"Is she passing away, here?"

"Yeah."

"Or … being taken to a hospital?" Peter asked.

"No."

"We're sitting in the moment, here, right now. That's what she's reliving. It's almost like that's her escape. Death is her escape and she's kind of locked herself into that place where she can't escape. Penance. Almost like a penance. You getting a penance there, Bonnie?" Carol asked.

"I'm getting a longing just to have it over."

"Yeah, but it's like it's … because that's what she's longing for, she's locked into the longing. That make sense?"

"Is she in any physical pain?" Peter asked.

"She's got a broken heart, but I don't know if that is literal or emotional. She's very thread-like, as if you can see through her hands. Like, paper-thin. You can see all her bones, all her knuckles, all her veins … and a very, very fine-boned … tiny person in the first instance. Oh! She was saying when she was young she was a beauty."

"Tell her she needs to hold that thought, Bonnie. That's what she needs to die with on her mind. She needs to change it to that, so let's just do that," Carol said.

"Yeah, okay."

"We can help her."

"And put her hair back up, instead of … she doesn't want it in a braid."

"Okay. So just see it, going back up. There, she just shifted a little bit, energetically. I just see herself … I see her like, dancing, a little bit. Yeah, so see her dancing when she was younger? And that's the thought that she needs to die with, so tell her as soon as she gets that thought in her mind, she can cross over."

"Perhaps she could tell us who she is so we could ..." Peter asked.

"She's laughing. She's showing me a man's hands around her waist and she's so tiny, he can span her. She's so little, but very delicate, very fine."

"Okay. So the energy has expanded. So she's actually crossed, at this point. So we'll get her back to ask her questions, okay? I just wanted to get her out of that state. We can always get them back."

"You want her back with a smile on her face, like she used to be."

"What we didn't want was her locked, so ..."

"Because you can't talk when they're locked. Like that one over there [referring to the grieving mother] couldn't talk to me because she was locked," Bonnie explained.

"Okay. So now you can talk to her. Just call her back in."

"Would she want to return if we called her back?" Peter asked.

"Just tell her that we want her to — you want her to — share some stuff. Peter would like you to come back ... and just share."

Bonnie started to hum. "She likes the song, 'Tea for Two.'"

"I hear the name Temperance."

"There's an Ann, too. There's a second Ann."

"The energy feels so much different in here. It's shifted and what happened was when there's that sadness there, it goes, "Wah," like this, and as soon as they get into a place of peace, it just goes, it expands right out. When I do Past Life work with people and I can get the past life to shift in that thought at that moment of death, it just opens way up and the person I'm working with and their heart just goes, 'Oh!'"

"She was beautiful. She was gorgeous."

"Very petite, though."

"Her name may be Ann?" Peter asked.

"There's an 'Annie' in there."

"Do you still see the bed?" Peter asked.

"Over there."

"Any idea of what era it's from?"

"It's iron and it's got a headboard."

"It's got iron — wrought iron, like an old ... rounded."

"Yeah. And not shiny. It's white, like somebody's painted it. But it's white, yeah. Just three loops. Sturdy," Carol said.

"Is she still here?" Peter asked.

"She's listening to me talk. She's laughing," Bonnie said.

"She can come and go now. She's not locked here."

"This wasn't her bed; she was brought here to this bed. But the quilt was hers. And the nightie was hers. At night, she looked like a child, she was so tiny. The nightie was hand-sewn with beautiful work in the bib. It's not bordelaise, it's not lace, but it's the raised needlework — it's knotted and it's raised."

"It sounds like embroidery," Peter added.

"It's like a type of embroidery and it's white-on-white and very, very fine linen. She's had it for a long, long time. And her wrists … the sleeves billow a bit and it looks like it's too big for her now. But it's hers. And it's very, very soft. She likes textures that are soft. But the quilt is hers. Yeah, that's what I'm getting."

"Do you want me to clear this room? Like, do you want all this energy in the house, or do you want stuff cleared? I mean, I had to clear that woman over there…." Carol asked the owner.

"She had to go," Bonnie stated.

"If this is someone in a better state of mind, I don't mind. I don't necessarily want her gone," the homeowner replied.

"You don't mind? Okay."

After moving some large living room chairs aside, Peter opened the door to the alcove under the stairs. Both mediums managed to squeeze into the space.

"I see a child cowering in the corner," Carol said, crawling back out of the closet. "I swear things like this were put together to hurt children."

"To punish them."

"Hm. I just see a child going back there. Like, out of sight, out of mind."

"A boy."

"Yup. Under five, eh?"

"Yeah, four. He actually likes to hide in here, 'cause that way they can't find him and make him work or do anything he doesn't want to do."

"But he gets put in there when he's bad!"

"Yeah, he gets put in here, but he doesn't mind that! He's not been beaten and thrown in, that's not what I get at all. He actually quite likes it."

"Well, you're looking very comfortable, Bonnie."

"Yeah. I can understand the feeling."

"He's like a monkey. He's a monkey!"

"What's your name, Monkey?" Peter asked.

"I didn't ask him. I just get, 'You little monkey!' That's all I get!"

"Is that something he would've been told?" Peter asked.

"Yeah, he was told, yeah. You little monkey! But there's nobody screaming at him, you know what I mean? It's like … kind of an exasperated mom who should be mad, but is laughing?" Bonnie exited the alcove. "And he just buggers off. He knows when he's pushed her buttons. He's cute!"

"Does he know his name?"

"I don't know! I just keep getting, 'Little Monkey.' They must've just called him that, constantly." Bonnie closed the alcove door. Did you get his name, Carol? I can't get his name. He was in mischief a lot."

"I know. I'm hearing 'Martin,' but I don't think that's his name."

"I think it's quiet.… I would've loved to have lived here," Carol added.

"Yeah, it's very cozy. It's very cozy. I don't feel threatened."

"I think it's Mark."

"Mark?" Peter asked.

"I think his name is Mark. I get 'Mark.' Not Marcus, just plain Mark."

"Who are your parents, Mark? You know your parents' names?" Peter asked.

"Martin."

"Martin. Mar-Mar-Mark. Okay."

"It's an 'M.'"

"It's a 'Mar' name."

"Mark, do you play downstairs, too?" Peter asked, referring to the crawlspace.

"Oh, he's cute. He's pure mischief, though."

They moved to the stairs and climbed up to the second floor.

"This is fear, what I'm feeling. This feels like somebody is being beaten. I would say kind of abused. That's what it feels like," Carol said immediately.

"Male or female?"

"It's a woman being abused. It's like she's like this" — Carol posed, crouched, forearms crossed over her head in self defense — "This space would've been different back in that time, and it feels like this was a regular thing."

Bonnie joined Carol on the landing. "Is it Mark's mom?" she asked.

"I'm going to say: good possibility."

"Do you feel her shaking?"

"Um-hm. Oh, she's terrified."

"Is she afraid of us?" Peter asked for clarification.

"This very much could be an impression, because whenever I come across abuse, it comes to me quickly, and if you don't clear it, it becomes part of the fabric of the home," Carol explained.

"Do you think that's the case now? You think that it's already become part of the fabric?" Peter asked.

"That's what it feels like."

"It's like another layer."

"It's like fabric … against it. It's just like fabric."

[Peter's digital recorder captures a dull thud followed by a louder one.]

"The guy who hit her, his name started with 'R.'"

[The recorder captures a loud cracking sound, like wood on wood smacking together. Then there is a light exhale and a female voice very gently saying, "Get out."]

"Is this part of the original home? Or this area here, only? Right?" Carol inquired of the owner.

"No, the whole thing was part of the original cottage."

"Oh, was it? This is a heck of a big cottage!"

"This was originally the loft. It's a good size, but this would've been the loft."

"Okay. It was more of a sleeping loft."

"Yeah. Back then there were three bedrooms here. We made it just one big room, put a washroom in, and then this little room. So it was quite different. There wasn't much up here before. You could see through the walls. They were just small pieces of wood. They were there just to make a divider. They weren't meant for privacy, and it wasn't fancy up here, by any means. It wasn't nice looking."

"There's a 'T' in this guy's name," Bonnie interrupted.

"R.T.?" Peter reaffirmed.

"Yeah, R.T."

"Is this a first name?" the owner asked.

"R is the first name. T is the second name."

"Is he here, too, or is she telling you?" Peter asked.

"He's standing behind and he's only showing me two initials. And he's a dark figure."

"And there is a spirit, right here." Carol gestured to the floor of the second-floor landing. "What I'm getting from her, it's like, all of a sudden we bore witness to her pain. And for her, that was important; she's been waiting for somebody to believe."

"Yeah, because it's like a secret shame. Probably a pillar of the community; you would never guess, like "fur coat and knickers," that whole thing about appearing to be one thing but being something completely different."

"I've never heard that expression before but I totally understand," Peter said.

"But it really feels like she just needed somebody to know the truth."

"It's validated," Peter said reassuringly.

"Yeah, so we've just validated her. So for her, you guys have helped fulfill a need that she's had for many, many, years. Now she says, 'I can be at peace.'"

"Okay, there's an 'I' here. And his name, he's showing me an 'I,' but very reluctantly. And he won't show me his face," Bonnie reported.

"Is he angry we're here?" Peter asked.

"Yeah. He's mad at being exposed. I said, 'Tough noogies,'" Bonnie said.

"We've met him," Peter said.

"Have you met him? Has he come across nasty to you, too?"

"Angry."

"He likes to use his fists, he likes to be seen as strong and — what's the word?"

"Macho?"

"Macho! But inside, he's a coward. And she knows it and so does he, but this is the big, dark secret. Nobody who met these people or knew them would ever believe that this was going on."

"Behind closed doors," Peter added.

"Yeah."

"Has she spoken out before?" Carol inquired.

"We think so, yeah. But not as much as we would like her to, ma'am. We would love to hear your story, so we can help," Peter said out loud.

"Well, we can clear it for her; I'm not worried. Clearing stuff is sort of my thing. I don't have a problem clearing that."

"I'm interested in knowing two things. Whether this man is a husband or a fiancé and what his name is, please," Peter asked.

After a long pause Bonnie exclaimed, "Oh boy!"

"He knows us. I know you do, sir. I use the term, loosely, because I don't approve of what you've been doing. We're no strangers; we've encountered each other many times," Peter said.

"She's saying she blamed herself for falling for the image. She bought into the image. And the reality was very, very different. So I would say they were married and the first time —" Bonnie told them.

Carol decided to move away from the short staircase railing, for safety. "I'm going to move away from here! I get the feeling he's going to push me or something!"

"Yeah, he's mad. The first time he back-handed her, she's saying she should've left him. That's what she's saying. Like, she protected his image and she suffered. She's angry at herself for not saying, 'You can't do that' and walking."

[On Peter's digital recorder are the sounds of a male panting, almost seething].

"Is your husband a public figure?" Peter asked.

"I'm getting he is somebody in the community."

"Yeah. I'm getting suit and tie."

"Period?"

"I'd say 1930s, just by the cut of the suit and the type of collar and the shirt. Sideburns. Hair brushed back. A bit to the side, but brushed straight back. Fancied himself a ladies' man is what I see."

"Does it make you happy to abuse women? Do you feel stronger?" Peter asked.

"He does it when he's drinking. He has an alcohol problem. There's like a funny taste in my mouth and I don't drink, so I can't figure out that taste. It's like a scotch? It's something you would drink 'neat,' pretty well, because it's got that taste that kind of lingers right on your tongue."

"Is he here?"

"Yeah, he's here."

"Yeah, he's a drinker. And he's got the complexion, like …"

"I think that what he was drinking was when he got…. He's standing over there, now."

"Oh right, yeah. Sort of ruddy?" Peter asked for clarification.

"Yeah. And the nose. The nose isn't too bad yet, but the cheeks give away the story."

"But I think his abuse gets heightened when he drinks."

"Yeah, which is common. You lose your inhibitions."

"He's got big, big hands. So I would say he probably works with the land or works with his hands, as well."

"Did you get the name, 'Carter'? Carter …" Carol blurted out.

"I was trying not to get that …"

"Because?" Peter asked

"Carters are affiliated with this whole area. Yeah, I know, so I have to shut up because I don't know if I'm prejudiced …"

"See, I was getting 'Carter' over there."

"Because I don't trust myself with names."

"I don't know if you hear the way I hear, but I only hear part of it and every once in a while, I just get a name. And then I can't find the person that it attaches to," Carol said.

"Okay, well I'm going to stand firm on the name 'Carter.'"

"Okay. May I ask him one more thing?" Peter asked.

"Uh-huh."

"Is he able to leave this property … and travel? 'Cause I want to ask you if you've followed me home," Peter said.

"Ah!" Carol said.

"I get, 'Hell, no.' But that could be a lie. He's a liar, he's a cheat, he's …" Bonnie said.

"What kind of problems have you had at your house?" Carol inquired.

"He likes to make people uncomfortable," Bonnie said.

"And he likes to plant doubt," Carol said

"I've seen like a … a shadow. Like, I don't see a physical body, sometimes like you see of spirit. I'm seeing more of a shadow. And I'm seeing like … threads. So it's almost like if he was standing here," Peter said.

"Thought forms," Bonnie said.

"Yeah, it could be thought forms,"Carol said.

"You know what? When we're finished, we'll clear him. We'll clear him when we finish this," Bonnie suggested to Peter.

"Yeah, we'll clear you."

Everyone moved into the master bedroom.

Bonnie commented, "I'm getting cold when I go in this room. I get really cold."

"Interesting, you get cold, I get hot," Carol said, laughing and moving to the south end of the room. She paused while Bonnie checked out the north side, near the bathroom.

Carol moved to Bonnie's side. "Oh. Yeah. That's all I'm picking up: Swept in a corner, for lack of a better term."

Bonnie moved into the bathroom for a short time, then called to Carol, asking, "Did somebody get stabbed?" Carol joined Bonnie in the bathroom while Peter followed to record from the door. "Did somebody get stabbed? Feel that, under my left shoulder blade."

"Right there, you sure it's a stab, or somebody whacked you on the back?"

"I'm stabbed. That wide." Bonnie indicated a two-inch blade using her thumb and forefinger.

"There's a real funny taste with it. Mmm. Can you move out?" Carol said.

"Oh yeah, I'm coming out!"

"You feel it, though. I can taste it."

"Blood. Two-inch blade it is, like a big butcher knife, or something. Did anybody die in this house?"

"Yeah, scores of people died in this house!" the owner stated.

"We know the baby died in here. The old lady died in here."

"We got the baby ..."

"John? What was his name? John?" Carol inquired.

"And we had ... whatever this is. This [knife stab] is in the back. But it's not a stab wound like this." Carole gestured stabbing over-handed. "It's a stab wound like this." She demonstrated an underhand thrust of a knife.

"How big was the blade?"

"At least two inches wide at the base of the blade. Like, it's a big, wide blade."

"I'm seeing like a short, sturdy, hunting knife."

"Any idea if this is our friend out there on the landing?" Peter asked.

"Could be. But you did all the talking to him, though!"

"Told you he was mad ... at you."

"Ugly soul."

"And that's why I got away from that stairs. I had a funny feeling that someone was going to push me."

"Push you over, yeah."

"Do you know what the sex of the victim, is?" Peter asked.

"I just got anger and a stab wound right up under the shoulder blade. Definitely an upward thrust and it's a male who did it, 'cause you'd have to have the strength to drill it through."

[On the digital recorder a male voice whispers, "Collar!" or "Call her!"]

"It's gone now," Bonnie stated.

"He was a very chaotic and bitter man, he was."

"Now, is this the same man you think from the landing?' the owner asked.

"I think it was."

"Yeah, it's almost like I'm getting … I'm hearing the words, 'Reign of Terror.' So I have a funny feeling …"

"I was getting, 'Reign of Terror.' But even in his business, he wasn't physically abusive like he would be here. He was not a kind man. He was a very angry man."

"And when he showed me the letters, they came up in bright red, against the black background."

"I'm hearing … I heard, 'Reign of Terror.'"

"Well, let's get rid of that bugger. He's got to go," Peter said.

Everyone returned to the second-floor landing.

"Is he all over the place? Is he retreating from you when you walk, or do you pick up parts of him as you go, or?" Bonnie asked.

"For me, it's almost as if … I think we're still getting different levels in this house, okay? So it's almost like I don't know whether this is a child over here, but I'm getting smaller energy that is not either well or happy, or …" Carol explained.

"Just is."

"It's just … not good."

"Like a throwaway child, you mean?"

"Yeah."

"Not Mark?" Peter inquired.

"No."

"It doesn't feel like Mark. Mark has a mischievous energy. He's playful. That's why I asked if he takes the caps off your paints, or does something … like if a thumb print got put on one of your paintings and you couldn't figure out where the thumb print came from. It's like a mark? A finger mark?"

"He's a little monkey! He really is!"

"He's very mischievous; very smart, but mischievous. This one here is more like … like a mousy little girl. Does that work? Mousy little girl." Carol asked.

"Yeah, that's what I got. I just got, 'Mouse, mouse hiding.'"

"Yeah. So there's that energy."

"And this is the bully."

"There's something over here, so I don't know whether they slept in this room at one time, or what. But there's that energy there."

"Is she their daughter? Is there a connection between abused spouse, him, and …" Peter asked.

"She really protected the little guy and the little girl used to just disappear," Bonnie explained.

"She's like one of those kids who could just fade into the woodwork and you wouldn't see her. Like, out of sight, out of mind."

"Is she his?"

"I have to say — emotionally she saw a lot. She lived in fear, so she would just make herself scarce, when she had to. 'Cause she was quite young, too. I think she might've been younger than Mark. Around like, two?"

"Two or three. Yeah, I get three."

"Three? See, I mean, they're close in age. But she's almost like —"

"Stepping stones."

"She's almost invisible. So … that was her energy, there."

"I think that's why she protected herself. If she was quiet, they didn't know where she was."

"Like a mouse."

"Yeah, like a mouse."

"So I would say one of these energies you want to keep in here. You know, if you're having a studio in here and a gallery, you want people to come in and you want them to stay. You don't want them walking in and walking out real fast; you want them to linger."

"But they do, though. That's the irony," Peter said.

"That's very ironic."

"Really?"

"They come in and they don't want to go," the owner told them.

"That's interesting."

"Uh-huh. It's true. I've seen it," Bonnie stated.

"Bonnie has been here and she had that feeling too, when she was visiting. And we sat in the studio, well; a few times you were here. You'd get that feeling."

"Uh-huh. But I white-light myself when I walk into this building," Bonnie stated.

"But not everybody does, so that's interesting that we pick up all this other negative-type energy."

"The thing is too, that when I had the gallery opening, we couldn't get people out of here after. I mean, they were reluctant to go!" the owner said.

"There is an overall feeling in here of joy. And I find when the more people there are in this house, the better. Now I don't know why that would be."

"It could be too that, you know, when you come in, we came in with a purpose. And our intention was to seek out spirits and the energies that do not work for your highest interest. And that's what we're finding. People coming in, they're seeking visual joy and expression through your paintings, which is what they get."

"And it's quaint and it's cute."

"Not everybody is as sensitive as Bonnie and I are to these negative-type energies."

"You see, it's definitely the negatives that I want gone. Especially when you're talking about fear and that woman's reaction. I don't want that in this building, at all. That is the lowest form of individual," the owner stated.

"Well, we can get rid of that. That's not an issue."

"But anything else, all the benevolent people that are here."

"People with good hearts and good intentions, yeah …"

"I don't care if they have a reason for being here. I don't really care."

"Somebody who was in this house loved to cook. All of a sudden I'm smelling cooking," Carol reported.

"Bread! Fresh bread!" Bonnie said.

"Cooking I can smell; it really smells nice and homey and stuff like that," Carol said.

"Mm. But you see you are picking up a lot of the negatives. Primarily the negatives," Bonnie said.

"Because that's easier for me to pick up," Carol said.

"That's definitely what I … yeah, I don't want that here," the owner said.

"But if you set your intention — like when you're coming to do something like this — we knew what we would be walking into some negativity. And we're both quite sensitive to that."

"Yeah, I agree," the owner stated.

"We work well together. But it's not the whole energy print of the place, at all."

"Yeah, I truly believe that's true. But this negative stuff is just not …"

"That has to go."

"For us it's like, seek and ye shall find!"

"Is he afraid to go? Do you think he stays because of that old standby that maybe he was religious and believes there's a Hell and he'll go there if he's crossed over?"

"Yeah, and least here he was in control. This was his mini-Hell for other people. But outside these four walls you never would've known."

"Still a little sick in that corner."

"Yeah, it's just … energy. Can we get rid of this guy?" Carol asked.

"Yeah, he's got to go."

"I'm going to send the lady to the light. They already know that they've died here, so …"

"That one? That mouse?"

"That's just an impression. I think in true hauntings, people see something and they don't stay long enough — if they're visual — to watch the whole thing and if it's totally repetitive that is definitely a residual energy pattern. That's just there, especially if you have a lot of old furniture. That brings in the energy and helps lock it down. But it was really more of a repetitive action, so it was more of an impression."

Peter jumped in sensing the window of opportunity to glean information was closing. "I'm wondering if we could ask this guy if there's anything he has to say to us before…. Or is that too much like an execution?"

"Maybe you'd better ask him, first."

"If he has any last words, or whether that's too execution-like? You're going to a better place, my friend. This is your last chance to let us know who you were in this life and clear your name. Do you want to be remembered as a monster? Or a coward? I don't think so," Peter said out loud.

"He got upset when you called him a coward," Bonnie said.

"Well then, you don't want to be remembered as that, do you? Please share with me your name before you find peace."

"I'm hearing he will come and tell you what his name is, afterwards. And he'll probably come in a dream. Do you dream? You may get his name in a dream tonight or tomorrow night. You'll have to let us know!"

"Okay, yeah. Should I be afraid, then?" Peter asked.

"No, once we cross them over, he's going to be totally transformed back into Pure Life and Love."

"I'm just checking! Thank you!"

Carol started, "So no fear! So we evoke the Violet Flame to come forth; twenty feet below, twenty feet around the property, this house and we ask that the Violet Flame lift and transmute all energies of those who are left behind who are in anger, grief, despair. We ask that you lift this up to the light. Transformation back to source, back to love."

Bonnie found the act of "lifting" the energies very "heavy." Peter reported feeling a heaviness around his solar plexus. Carol and Bonnie repeated the rite again.

"It's like they're going up in … pieces," Carol reported.

"He's heavy. He's really heavy; he feels like lead. Very resistant," Bonnie said.

"He can't resist it. I've no doubt!"

Carol and Bonnie performed a variation of the rite a third time. Afterward, they checked a couple of areas of the landing and quietly agreed there were still residual pieces left.

"We're going to do it one more time, because …"

"Part of him is still here?" Peter said.

"Threads."

"The threads are here of what he did to her and it's coming through as her whole upper body, especially her arms are aching from the blows he rained down on her. So we're just going to clear that last little bit, again."

Carol and Bonnie recited a variation of the Violet Flame ritual.

"Fill this house with light," Carol started.

"And peace," Bonnie continued.

"And we replace all fear and anger with that of love and joy. So the bones of this house now vibrate with love. There, that feels better. Can you feel the difference? Do you feel — I don't know how much you feel …" Carol finished.

"Not much. But the first time you did the raising of the arms, I felt something in my stomach. It could be lunch, but …" Peter said.

"Yeah. It's gone now, right?"

"No. It feels tight. It feels very tight, right now," Peter reported.

Carol showed Peter a relaxing stance, whereby the fingers on both hands are curled in meditation-like positions.

"You're very angry that this man hit this woman."

"He is? You're emanating it."

"Just let it go. It's not yours. You don't own it. And you don't want to give it any more life than what it had" — she paused — "There. Something just popped out of there. Do you feel better?"

The group headed back downstairs for a break.

"You know what you mentioned upstairs? That corner where you guys kept saying 'mouse'? I always thought it was a mouse making noise there because I used to hear noises. I used to say, 'we've got mice in the wall,'" the homeowner said.

"Yeah, well, it's a mouse, just a mouse of a different kind. That's a good affirmation Carol," Peter said.

Bonnie explained again how painful the stabbing feeling was.

"It's funny when you're talking about the knife. I wasn't seeing a long knife. It was almost like one of those … shucking knives?" Carol said.

Peter excused himself to retrieve the asparagus knife from the kitchen drawer.

"Was it something like this?" Peter asked, handing Carol the asparagus knife.

"Something like that, yeah. But the blade looked a bit bigger than that. Is this from this property?"

"Yes. Are either of you adept at psychometry?"

"Yeah, both of us."

Bonnie took off her ring and handed it to Peter to hold and then took the knife.

"Yes, thank you. I see a female, about five-foot-seven, bun on the back of her head, honey-blonde hair and when she worked in the kitchen she wore like a blue dress — it was her house dress, like a day dress — and she wore a white pinny on the top; it was a square white pinny. I know this was true! I see that she was left handed and she was very skilled at peeling with her left hand!"

"This isn't the same — younger version — of the woman you picked up in the northwest room?" Peter asked.

"No, no, this one's tall. She's about five-seven, this lady. And she's thin, but her hair is … she had beautiful hair, but she always pulled it back into a bun that sat right here. She seemed very happy."

"So this knife is something she used?" Peter asked.

"Prepping. She showed me potatoes and then she showed me carrots, and I'm going, 'How can you work so fast with your left hand?' She says, 'You adapt.' As I'm saying, 'Hey! You're left-handed!' She said, 'Yes.'

"Yeah, see, I don't know enough about knives, but she used to hold it like this." Bonnie gripped the handle and placed her thumb on the top-edge of the blade, for support. "See this thing here? Her thumb would rest here and she would work really, really fast. I couldn't believe it 'cause she's left-handed. But she says, 'You adapt,' so …"

Peter passed the pistol to Bonnie to read. She closed her eyes and sandwiched the gun between her hands.

"Was this found underground, near water?"

"No. Found underground? No," Peter said.

"Okay, but had it been underground near water at one point?"

"I don't know about the water part, but I don't think it was underground. It was hidden, but not underground."

"Okay. I think whoever had this should've buried it and let it rust and die, you know? In all fairness, I think this is a gun. Am I right?"

"I thought you would've picked that up simply by touching it."

"Well, see, because the owner has told me the odd thing, I've had to really blank my mind and then I have to blank my judgment, so it takes me a while to wrap and then I have to ask for permission if I can do this and will it fairly allow me to read it. Because I know that there was a pistol found on this property."

"Yes, okay, so you knew that ahead of time."

"Yes, that's why, number one, I usually look at an item before I do psychometry, but number two, because I knew what the owner had told me, I had to clear that. I almost said to you, no because I knew … in all fairness, I want to try and read it. There was a horse in kind of like a garage-barn combination. There were vehicles as well as a horse. Probably a tractor, but I see also an old car … maybe something from the late thirties? Car's black, left rear bumper had the light punched out of it, or something. Something hit it. Hmm, when this was found, was it wrapped in burlap?"

"I believe it was wrapped in —"

"Or rags?"

"Cloth, fabric of some kind."

"Okay. Yeah, I see like a dirty oil rag and then a burlap on top of that.

Probably. They should have buried it; they didn't want it found. And it's 'they' — it's two people who knew what this gun was used for."

"That's what we're curious about, too. Whether a crime was committed, or ..."

"Well, if you find a body on the property, I wouldn't be surprised!" Long pause. "You know what? I see barrels upon barrels, upon barrels, upon barrels."

"Rum-runners," Carol added.

"Are they in that same garage or shed, or whatever?"

"Yeah. I would not be surprised if there was some booze-smuggling going on during the depression, or whenever there was a ban on booze and we used to ship from Canada over the Great Lakes to Buffalo, Chicago. That was very common; that's how a lot of people survived through the Great Depression, running booze. Okay, I think it was kept on the property and I think this was used basically to guard, because enough people knew what was being run out of here and they used to ... one would sit guard. One would have to sit on guard, especially at night. That's what I see. The one guy that I'm seeing, light/dark tie and he had sparkles on it; red-green sparkles on a black tie. I could see that. I can see a guy in a hat. They were short; the two guys were quite short."

"Are they from here?"

"No."

"From out of town?"

"Out of town."

"American?"

"They used to come in and arrange the pick-up."

"And you said 1930s-ish?"

"It feels like thirties-ish, looking at the fedora-type hat. And only the one guy wore a hat, interestingly enough. The other guy didn't even want to take a ... like they used to put a mac on over their suits. He didn't even want to do that in case they had to run. It's what I'm hearing him say to the other guy."

"Are they exchanging names?"

"They are almost like brothers; they know each other very well and they can read each other really, really well."

"No, I'm just curious who would've owned the property — at that point — that they would probably know."

"I'm just watching what they're doing. It's a name with an 'S,' that's all I know. The reason I asked if this spent time in water, is because at one point they were carrying a shipment and they had to hide it in water. I don't know if they dropped it down a well or if it was a deep pond on whatever property, but it's almost like they wrapped this and put this in the water, too, so they wouldn't get caught. This — I'm sure — has spent time in water."

"Uh … it may have become wet after it was hidden and wrapped and moisture may have gotten to it, because it's quite rusted. I've cleaned some of it off, trying to get a serial number, but there isn't any on there," Peter said.

"Probably filed off."

"I thought so too, but it must be expertly done, because there isn't even a groove left over from filing. But that's not to say when they were manufactured, that some of them could have left the assembly line without a number."

"Absolutely."

"These were so popular, this particular brand, here," Peter said.

"It's like a Saturday Night Special, eh?" Carol said.

"I don't know what they looked like, but this is a British Bulldog," Peter said.

"The guy who held this had a very thick bottom lip. Very protruding bottom lip," Carol said.

"You get a sense that it was ever used to kill someone, or more like a warning or a threat?" Peter asked.

"More of a warning, to scare people. Isn't that funny? It was almost like he — the guy who used it — used to wave it around. It was almost like he was more afraid of the gun than any damage the gun could do," Carol said.

"We're just wondering why it was hidden, whether it was from authorities, or if it wasn't used to kill someone or harm somebody. Why hide it? That's part of the mystery," Peter said.

"You know what it could be, one of those things where the cops were close and they just hid and lit out? It could very easily be that. 'Cause this gun's done a lot of travelling. You know, it's interesting, I wonder if the guy who used this was actually an ex-cop, because he used to carry it in the back — like, not in his back pocket — he'd carry it back here, by his right kidney. He kept it right in the back; I can feel it, it's weird. Okay, feel how warm this is, now. When I took it, it was ice-cold," Carol said.

"You can see on the top, it says, British Bulldog," Peter said.

"Did it really work?! Oh, yeah. Very cool," Carol said.

"And we think it's British in origin, so when you say travelled ..." Peter said.

"Yeah. Oh, this went back and forth on booze runs, all the time," Carol said.

"I think you had some rum-runners on your property!" Bonnie told the owner.

"This guy was very confident, 'cause a loaded gun in your back belt pointing right toward your butt?! He had to be confident! I just wonder if he was ex-military or ex-police. This is really cool!"

"That's an interesting take, as well," Peter said, thinking about the military angle.

"Well it's just that he's so adept at handling it."

Carol took the pistol in her hands. "This has killed somebody."

"You think so? It's been fired. Do you think it did kill somebody?" Bonnie asked.

"Un-huh. I can feel him shooting somebody and feeling ... Gotcha! Just like, no remorse, whatsoever! So I think this was owned by one of the bad guys, for some reason. Yeah, how can you call somebody a bad guy for trying to mix some booze, right?"

"Is it hard to tell where that would've been fired, then? Whether it was on the property, or on a run, or something like that?" Peter asked.

"If you walked around, would you be able to locate the spot where it was fired?" the owner asked.

"We might be able to."

"Should we take it with us?"

Carol looked at Bonnie. "Why don't you wear it in your pocket? Carry it in your pocket?"

"I'll put it in the back, like he did!"

"That gun won't fire anyway, any more!"

"No, I know, I mean, she already got stabbed in my bathroom!" the owner said.

"That's true!" Carol said, laughing.

"That bloody hurt! I did not like that."

"Well, you know, you piss someone off, you expect to be ..."

"Whoa! I white-lighted myself; I didn't expect him to be able to get through!"

"He was pretty powerful in his anger."

"He was nasty!"

[As everyone dresses in their winter coats the digital recorder picks up a raspy voice saying, "Ready-ready! Ready!"]

They moved across the property and entered the barn.

"First impressions?" Peter asked.

"Terror. Not fear. Terror," Carol stated immediately.

"Terror."

"As soon as you walk in?" Peter asked.

"Well, I'm looking for it, right?" They stopped at the ladder to the loft. "Do we have to go up there?"

"Uh-uh, no," Bonnie said.

"We won't go up. No, I don't go up things like that. We'll just stay here ..."

"It's actually very safe to walk," Peter told them.

"Is it?" Carol shuddered as the group moved into the storage area. "I'm going to tell you what I got when you sent me that young man's photo: when I look at him I can't breathe, so that tells me he's dead. And I just felt something with my throat. It was just like a constriction, and it just got tighter and tighter. I just know that's how he expired. I had the sense that either he was killed on this property, or that he was left on this property after he died. That's all I can tell you about that. And that's what I'm feeling in this barn, is that terror."

"Are we talking garrote?" Bonnie asked.

"Yeah. That's what I was getting."

"Revenge?"

"I don't know what the purpose was. To me there's no good purpose for it."

"No. That's why I'm wondering if it was a revenge killing. Getting back at his family."

"Well, I'm feeling it might have something to do with drugs. But I'm not positive."

"Okay."

"That's from the photo?" Peter inquired.

"Yeah."

"Do you feel him here? As we stand?"

"I think he's why I don't want to go up."

"Well, I don't know ... he hung himself? Maybe he hung himself; I keep getting around the throat."

"I'm getting this again. This anxiety."

"I'm not sure he didn't hang himself. Do you know the story?" Bonnie asked Peter.

"So, do you know anything? Was he dead?"

"I don't know."

"You don't know. Nobody knows."

"That's what we're trying to find out. I'm more interested — as always with me — in names, an era, and if we can verify him in the picture with historical fact," Peter explained.

"Well, when I was working off the picture, that's what I was getting. Like, when I go in to see if somebody's alive or dead — if somebody's asking, 'alive or dead' — I bring their energy into my body. Not the greatest thing to do, but that's what I do. And if I can still breathe, I know they're alive! If I go like this, then I know they're dead; then they go away real fast. But I really got him out of there and I just feel this tightness around my throat. So garroting, it could be somebody doing this, or it could be a strangulation, hanging themselves because it would have the same effect."

"So you got that feeling more in here than anywhere else?" the owner asked.

"Yeah, I got this absolute fear, in here."

"When you open that door."

"Yeah. And I'm feeling like I want to cry. Sorry, the tears are running."

"I wasn't sure; I thought it was cold that caused watery eyes."

"No, no, it's really …"

"Abject terror."

"So I can't tell you for sure whether he just hung himself. A lot of people who go to that point, they change their mind and then, it's like it's too late."

"This is for real."

"Yeah, 'cause he wasn't very old."

"I picture thirteen, maybe."

"Yeah, I put him a little older than that, but not much, so …"

"As you can see, we don't always agree on everything."

"That's fine," Peter said.

Peter pointed out that even the investigative team had varying opinions on the boy's age, especially since only half his face was seen in the frame of the picture.

"Huge anxiety."

"I'm just shaking here."

"It's huge!"

"Yeah, it's fear."

"I can relax enough if I'm cold. I don't get cold any more. I'm going to say that it's a guess, but it's a pretty good educated guess. I think he actually was killed."

"He didn't commit suicide?" the owner asked.

"I have my doubts. There's just too much fear. I'm almost seeing two people coming at him."

"Where's the body?"

"Do you know what his name is?"

"No," Peter told them.

"You don't know what his name is?"

"We would like to know."

"Where is the boy in the picture? Where are you?" Bonnie asked out loud.

"Are you in this building?" Carol asked.

"He wanted to disappear. How old is the floor?"

"Pretty old."

"Okay."

"He says, 'Yes,'" Carol said.

"Yes what?" Peter asked.

"He's in the building. That's why I asked you about the floor."

"Now, that could be in one of two ways: The physical body could be here, or the spiritual body could be here because this is where he was killed and then they took the body somewhere else. So the spirit body would stay here, where it happened."

"The floor is old, but if you want to come walking around here?" the owner asked them.

"See, I thought this floor was a little more recent than that floor because it was built up," Peter said pointing to the floor.

"Oh yeah, that's true, it is."

"Show me where you are. Show me where you are," Carol said.

Carol walked back into the stable area, following her dowsing rods, and discovered the entrance to the cellar.

"There's a basement? Is there a light down there?"

"Yes, there is."

They turned on the light and followed Peter as he descended into the cellar.

"What was here?" Carol asked upon seeing the dirt mound in the cellar floor.

"That's what we're going to find out. We don't know."

"Right there."

"Not even the owners know," Peter said.

"Because that feels like something."

"We thought so, too."

"Try the back corner," Bonnie said.

"Yeah, I know, just a minute," Carol said, trying to concentrate.

"Sorry." Bonnie moved toward the northeast corner as Carol concentrated on her L-rods poised over the mound. She whispered a question.

"Where are you? Uh … possibly right here."

"Un-huh. Well it is human-shaped," Peter added.

"Well, there is a bit of a lump here. Do you have a ground-penetrating radar person?"

"No."

"The owners gave us permission to dig, when the frost lets up."

"Okay, this is where the rods are pointing, Bonnie. I want to go in clearer, okay? Is there another body over there? Are there more?"

Peter pointed out the mummified cat skeleton in the dirt.

"Oh, then we're going to get two bodies, for sure."

"Say, human bodies?" Peter asked.

Carol began asking her L-rods. "How many bodies, please? One … two … three. How many human bodies are buried in here? I heard one … two …" she said as the L-rods swayed back and forth, searching. "Okay, I just want a number; human bodies, please. One … okay, there's one there." She indicated the mound. "Okay, show me again, show me others." The rods didn't move for a time.

"Do you want to walk over there, maybe?" Peter asked.

Carol and Peter walked toward Bonnie in the northeast corner.

After a moment of silence, Carol said, "It's not giving me a clear answer. It … it keeps pointing over this way." She indicated back toward the mound. "That's where my sense pulled me over to as soon as I walked in here. Which kind of validates …"

"Well, it's raised."

"Well, I get here, too," Bonnie said.

"Right here?"

"I mean, this would make a great burial spot."

"It would."

"Who'd even think to look here?"

"What I'm concerned about: was there more than one boy missing from this area?"

"That's what I get. I get … I get a body here, definitely."

"Oh, I get so much fear for this guy. I can see him crouching and in total fear."

"So you would agree that there's a very good possibility?" Peter asked.

"There are two areas, so …" Carol stated.

"I get two, potentially."

"Potentially?"

"Potentially two, yeah."

"So I'm calling him, 'Boy in the picture,' 'cause I could see the picture."

"If 'boy' could tell us his name, or give us an indication as you're calling him 'boy,' he might object to …" Peter said.

Bonnie marveled at the various newspapers lining the ceiling of the cellar. "How old is this?"

"1917."

"This energy just shifted," Carol reported.

"How?"

"They may have moved the body, but if you find something down there, I would love to know, because all of a sudden he's just feeling better. He's feeling happy that he's been found; that he understands that somebody has found him. That they know about him now."

"They were storing asparagus here," the owner told them.

"Were they?"

"Yeah, the last owner. And gladiolas. That's why the generator was here, to keep it cool. And when we purchased the property, the owners said we should grow mushrooms here. He kept saying this would be a great place to grow mushrooms."

"If he's here with us, and you're feeling better, would you let us know how you arrived here?" Peter asked.

"It's sort of like, against my will."

"Obviously, yeah. And I feel sorry that you're here; I'm sure we all do. Would you like us to take steps to extract you from here?" Peter asked.

"You know, I'm getting … it's almost like he is feeling … 'Somebody knows where I am and I'm okay now.' Because when you start to extract, you change the energies again for him."

"Do you know who your killers were?" Peter asked, still looking for answers.

"Bonnie, why don't you ask that one?" Carol suggested.

"He's saying, 'No.'"

"You can't name your murderers?"

"He's saying, 'No.'"

"How many were there?" Peter asked.

"Two."

"Are they still in this barn?" Peter asked.

"I'm getting they were brothers. Does that make sense?"

They both started to laugh. Peter looked at them.

"Yes! He says, 'I don't know, I'm dead!'"

"It's good to have a sense of humour."

"Do you remember your name, then? That's very funny. What's your name?"

"Come on lady, 'I'm DEAD.'"

"What was your name, then?" Peter asked, becoming frustrated.

"I get Ricky."

"How old were you, Ricky, when you died?"

"I think fifteen," Carol said.

"I get thirteen. But I've always got thirteen. The first time I saw this picture I got thirteen; it doesn't mean I'm right. It's just what I got," Bonnie stated.

"I think he saw something he wasn't supposed to see, basically," Carol said.

"He knew something," Bonnie added.

"He just happened to be at the wrong place at the wrong time, saw something and that was not good," Carol said.

"Were you staying in the loft, when you were found?" Bonnie asked.

"They grabbed him … by the arms … and lifted him. I can tell you that. They heard him and they grabbed him. He knew they meant business," Carol said.

"Do you remember having your picture taken by my friend, a couple months ago, in the loft? Was that you?" Peter asked.

"All I'm seeing is a pair of eyes and he's looking right at you. They just turned and went, I see you. That's what he's doing. I see you."

"Well, thanks to that photograph, I think we see you, too. Was that you?" Peter said.

There was a noise behind them.

"Carol, don't move, it just started here and it's walked across here, on the leaves, crunching."

"Ricky, I can't hear you. But this little machine I'm holding might be able to hear you. Could you please shout something into it? Can you tell me your surname? Your last name, please? Go ahead and shout it into this device, please. Shouting won't hurt it and it won't hurt you. That would be very helpful, if you could tell us the year you died," Peter said.

There was a long pause.

"We may even try to find who killed you. Did you hear something, upstairs?" Peter asked.

"I think it's the wind. The wind picked up. Yeah, it's just the wind," Carol said.

"I can hear tapping, but I thought I heard a voice. Like, the lower register of a male's voice, talking. Was that you? Clicking?" Peter asked.

"That's the sound I heard."

"It was behind me."

"Where there's no wind. But interesting that it's only started to do that. We've been here a few minutes and didn't hear any of that," Peter noted.

"I'm inviting it to channel through me. He's not doing it, yet," Carol said. "He's having a hard time coming through. I'm hearing 'Parker' and also the word 'perish.'"

"Which could be two different things, couldn't it? Dying or the church," Peter noted.

"That's what my feeling was."

"A thirteen- or fifteen-year-old might not use the word 'perish' when thinking of dying," Peter explained.

"Ah, it's stuck in my throat, come on …!"

"Is somebody stopping you from speaking to us?"

"I think he's just been silent for too long."

"Are you happy that we're addressing you? That we found you? You don't need to be alone. Some of us will come back. You don't need to be alone."

Pause.

"Is someone stopping you from communicating with us?" There was another pause, longer this time. "Are they here in the room, too?"

"Are they in the barn?"

"Were you killed in the loft?"

"Were you hanged?"

"Or were hands used to strangle you?"

"Do you remember what year that happened? When you died?"

"Whether it was summertime? Spring? Winter?"

Peter stopped his EVP session and looked to Carol.

She shook her head, nothing.

"I can't talk," Carol said.

"He's not talking," Bonnie stated.

"It's like he's gagged," Carol said.

"Well, thank you if you did answer and did speak into this device. God bless and we'll visit you again," Peter said.

Everyone started moving, ready to exit the cellar.

"Are you sure that's the boy that's missing?" Bonnie asked.

"That's what we're trying to find out," Peter answered.

The group made its way back to the house as the weather worsened and the temperature dropped.

"It takes a fair amount of energy to do that, as you know," Bonnie said.

"I can appreciate that."

"I wouldn't mind coming back and doing the loft, but I would want to do it separately."

"And in better weather, too."

"Well, that doesn't bother me. I feel really, really ... like, my stomach's on fire and that's unusual for me."

They entered the cottage and started to talk again about the photo of the boy.

"Believe me, we tried to debunk it as best as we could," Peter explained going through the entire process.

Carol interrupted and said, "He just said, 'You got me! You got me!' That's what I'm getting: 'Got me!' He's excited!"

"Well, we brought this picture up there before and asked him his name. Somebody else thought his name was Mark."

"We're getting a Mark around here a lot! This house has so many names attached to it, that they get into the fabric. So you get anybody who's intuitive or psychic or whatever term you want to use and you're going to start picking up all the same names. Sometimes you just can't attach them to the specific body of what you're looking at. I think he saw something he was not supposed to see and they weren't taking any chances. I mean, those people were pretty brutal."

"Well, yeah, if they had a vested interest and they're doing that to protect themselves."

[The digital voice recorder picks up a loud snapping sound, like the crack of a piece of wood.]

The owner and Peter thanked the mediums for all their work and effort and offered to keep in touch.

Conclusions:

- We picked up a "John" in the dining room of the cottage, who had allegedly died young from a fall from a horse or a tractor.
- We picked up on an anguished female rocking and eternally holding a dead child, and on the abusive relationship of a husband to wife in the cottage second storey landing. Initials R., T., I. were given by the male spirit.
- We picked up on an elderly woman in the northwest ground-floor room.
- We picked up on a young boy named "Mark" who used the crawl space under the cottage stairs to hide from his parents, but would also get locked up inside as punishment. (This may be significant as Joan picked up on the name "Mark" in this same area and associated it with the blow-up photo of Barn Boy at the time.)
- It became inexplicable when several independent mediums started to describe similar or even the same names and events that were all linked to this particular property, all without ever meeting or communicating with each other.

A Note on Mediums and "Clearings"

I had never before worked on a case where the client brought in their own mediums, though I did find it interesting to see what they had to say and compare it to what we had collected from our own mediums and electronic voice phenomena. I had to admit that after looking at all the data, I was very concerned. The secondmost concerning thing was the report of these little grey creatures with dark hair and black eyes that were attempting to look like children. Could these creatures exist? None of my team had seen them. From their description, they sounded similar to demonic entities that are referred to as "black-eyed kids." Even though we had not seen them, it was difficult for me to discount their existence because my team and I had encountered odd phenomena both in the barn and within the house. The smell of feces, for example, came and went as if attached to something passing by unseen. Our list of questions grew: What were they? What were their intentions? What was their purpose in being here?

After working the location for almost six months, I found myself torn between believing it may be something evil and just something else unknown at that time. Nonetheless it was unnerving that these things possibly existed and had been moving all around us while we did our investigations.

But the most concerning thing was that there was something larger lurking unseen, waiting in the background. I mention this as something I have seen in the past on another investigation. It could have all the appearances of a typical haunting but could actually be a diabolical trap. I am not saying this is what we were dealing with, just that the possibility exists.

In a great deal of diabolical hauntings, there are common elements. One being the draw of people to a particular place, normally a home. It always begins with feeling an immediate and unexpected attachment to a dwelling — perhaps "love it at first sight." Many people had observed that this property had a very distinct allure for passersby, who feel they simply must enter.

When this observation was coupled this with the yet unidentifiable grey entities, roving stench, and paranormal activity, all the elements of a trap were present. We also had to keep in mind that one of our mediums was physically attacked and that there had been visitations at our own private residences. Added into the equation was that the place was originally a church with the hint of abuse, missing persons, and possibly murder, and there was more than enough to mean that a holy place had been desecrated. Might that make this the perfect location for something truly evil to nest?

The next question I asked myself was: Should we take the information that we had and move on? Or do we press on and dig even deeper? It felt a little like we were about to poke a hornets' nest with a stick and then wait to see what might happen.

Some mediums feel the need to "clear" spirits from a location. We the living like things to be done quickly and efficiently — who wouldn't want a spirit removed from the home we live in? Most haunted properties, however, have more than one resident spirit and there is normally a mix of malevolent and benevolent spirits existing in some sort of balance.

When a well-wishing medium comes in and clears those spirits that are easy to clear, they may even attempt to clear the difficult ones. They tell you "mission accomplished," and walk away with a smile and sometimes a fistful of your money. But then things can take a turn for the worse, for the balance has been shattered. The good, or "easy," spirits are gone, and the malevolent spirits given free reign over you and your home. In the case of this property, I was extremely concerned about the clearing that took place.

10

FIFTH INVESTIGATION
LATE MARCH

Peter, Paul, Victoria, and I arrived on-site and parked near the barn. After setting up our surveillance equipment in the cottage and bringing Victoria up to speed on some recent events, we decided to head out to the barn.

I felt it would be a good idea to set up a surveillance system in the loft of the barn. We placed the system in the far corner in an attempt to get the best view possible of the entire space. Once the system was operating, the team headed back to the cottage.

I noticed a large television set sitting in the studio on the main floor and I suggested that later we could try some experiments with an ITC session. The team examined the television to ensure it worked, which it did.

Peter activated the recorder and approached the trapdoor to the crawl-space. Paul commented on the painting on the wall over the trapdoor, recognizing the figure in it as Jesus Christ with his cross across his shoulders. Peter added, "And a soldier, behind him."

[Immediately there is a blast of static on Peter's digital voice recorder.]

Peter pulled the trapdoor open and descended into the crawlspace of the house, followed by Paul. Peter activated and placed the E. Probe on one table and the digital voice recorder partly obscured under a plastic bag on another table.

Peter and Paul headed back up to the main floor and Peter dropped the trapdoor, sealing his equipment in the crawlspace.

We agreed that it was time to break for some lunch, but because we had surveillance operating in the barn I felt it important to leave one person behind to watch over the equipment. Paul volunteered to stay and the rest of us headed out to pick up the food.

After standing and listening for ambient noise in the cottage, Paul exited the house, calling out for the benefit of the recording systems, "I'm leaving!" and closed the back door behind him. Around twenty minutes later, Paul re-entered the cottage and walked throughout the main floor asking questions aloud. He made his way up to the second storey.

[A pair of loud knocking sounds are recorded by the camera on the second floor.]

Paul started back down the stairs, wandering the rooms asking for Miriam before exiting the house and closing the back door behind him.

[There is a very subtle tick *sound near the recorder. Then a loud* snap *farther from the recorder, but on the ground floor.]*

We arrived back at the property with pizza and coffee and found Paul standing outside. Everyone re-entered the house to eat.

[Out in the barn loft, the surveillance camera captures a white light that lands near the hatch, blinks, and then vanishes.]

After eating, the four of us headed out to the barn. We entered and I pulled the door closed behind us and chained it. Peter headed up to the loft, while Paul and I inspected the main floor. Victoria went directly into the cellar and started an EVP session. Above us, Peter was also conducting an EVP session. Paul and I inspected the construction of the barn, looking for where they added to the original structure.

Victoria was asking questions about the cellar, about us preparing to dig, and if anything would be found. She paused as there came knocking in rapid succession, eight to ten knocks. She felt it might be us upstairs; so she knocked back and then came up to check with us.

"Did anyone knock up here?" she asked.

Paul and I looked at each other, "No, why?"

"There was a lot of knocking down there."

I moved to the bottom of the ladder of the loft. Looking up, I called to Peter, "Peter, were you banging up there?"

He appeared at the loft hatch. "No."

"Victoria said there was knocking down in the basement."

"Like, literally." She moved to a support beam and gave it five hard knocks to demonstrate the sound.

"And then I went like this back, I went" — she knocked a few more times — "I thought it was you guys."

Peter came down to the main floor.

In unison Peter and Paul said, "No."

"It was very clear!"

"We didn't hear that," I said.

"Yeah, like right above me! I thought you guys were joking!"

"Well, this is concrete! It's not even wood!" I explained, pointing to the floor where we were standing.

"Yeah, it was somebody walking. I heard footsteps walking and then *knock, knock, knock, knock, knock.* And not just one knock, but *knock, knock, knock, knock.*"

Peter volunteered to test for the sound of footfalls and headed down to the cellar.

We walked around to see if Peter could hear us, but he reported that he couldn't. We stomped on the floor and he started to hear us faintly. He returned to the main floor.

[The light in the loft returns.]

Victoria headed to the cellar alone again.

"Can you knock again?" Victoria asked.

There was an immediate response — a distant knock.

[Her digital voice recorder captures a woohoo.*]*

Peter heard the knocking as well. "Did you hear that?"

Neither Paul nor I heard it, even though we were standing near Peter.

[The surveillance camera in the loft captures a male voice on the microphone saying, "Better."]

As Victoria continued asking questions she heard distant knocks, and she headed back up to the main floor to join us. Everyone moved up the ladder into the loft.

[The camera records the light moving back and forth near the hatch.]

Peter and Victoria started to have a conversation about the ancient floor boards when Peter saw something pass the barn outside through gaps in the barn boards. There was a voice calling out, "Hey."

Peter moved to the side wall and opened a small door and looked out, finding no one.

We heard the very distinct creaky-hinges sound of the bar door opening.

"Who came in?" Paul asked.

"I don't know," I said, heading toward the hatch.

"I just saw something outside," Peter told us.

"I thought you chained the door?" Paul asked me.

"I did," I said, heading down the ladder. I got to the main floor to find that the door was as I left it, still chained shut.

[Light moves back to the hatch, then vanishes again.]

Peter came down and we looked around the main floor for any sign of someone there.

Paul and Victoria started down. Paul was standing on the ladder, halfway through the hatch still taking photos. Behind him, the surveillance camera was capturing activity.

["I want you to come here," says a male voice.

Two lights appear side by side near the hatch, inches away from Paul. The microphone detects undistinguishable whispers.

A male voice says, "Hey." Then more whispers, as if trying to get Paul's attention.]

Paul arrived on the main floor.

The place seemed to have gone quiet, and we decided to go back to the cottage and try a Spirit Box session.

[The camera captures what sounds like the barn door again and the lights return, moving closer to the loft hatch.]

We entered the cottage and moved into the studio on the main floor. I retrieved the Sprit Box from my kit and attached the speakers to it and turned them both on.

"Hello?" Peter began.

Immediately a voice over the speaker: "Re-mem-ber."

"How are you?"

Spirit Box — a male voice: "No!"

"Do you remember me?"

Spirit Box — "Jim ... two ... are ... laid."

Spirit Box — a female voice: "Don't!"

"I was here a couple of weeks ago. Do you remember me?"

There was nothing but static.

"R.T.I. Are you here?"

Spirit Box — a male voice: "I hope … McGregor … were here."

Spirit Box — a male voice: "No."

Spirit Box — a male voice, shouting: "Push … now … run!"

"Is that a yes? Do you remember me? Yes or no?"

Spirit Box — a male voice: "I'll bet … he didn't … come."

Spirit Box — a male voice: "Who?"

Spirit Box — a male voice: "The … man."

Spirit Box — a male voice: "Illegal!"

Spirit Box — a male voice: "Come here."

Spirit Box — a male voice: "You made it … from jail. New York."

There was nothing but white noise for twelve seconds.

"Who's here, right now?" I asked.

Spirit Box — a male voice: "Well I don't … remember … the …"

Spirit Box — a male voice: "What is it? Shh! Quiet."

"What's your name?" I asked.

Spirit Box — a male voice: "I'll tell … my name is … Cole."

Spirit Box — a male voice: "You all … get in … the room."

Spirit Box — a male voice: "I am … a crook!"

Spirit Box — a female voice: "Ha ha!"

Spirit Box — a male voice: "Jim."

Spirit Box — a male voice: "What? C'mon, boys."

"It sounds like answers that should be short are dragged on, for —"
Peter said.

"Yeah," I acknowledged.

"We don't understand you, sorry!" Peter said.

Spirit Box — a male voice: "Where'd they go?"

Spirit Box — another male voice: "What'd they do?"

Spirit Box — a male voice: "Oh boy."

Spirit Box — a male voice: "Burned."

Spirit Box — a female voice: "Again … we hide."

"Can you slow down your speaking?" Peter asked.

Spirit Box — a male voice, raspy sounding: "As you … wish?"

Spirit Box — a male voice: "Cloris!"

"Do you wish to speak to us?" Peter asked.

Spirit Box — a male voice: "We're all … dead."

"I'm going to go out to the barn," Paul said.

"Is it okay if we go to the barn to dig?" I asked.

There is nothing but white noise.

"Do you think we'll find anything if we dig in the cellar of the barn?" I inquired.

Spirit Box — a male voice: "Leave …"

Spirit Box — a male voice: "Here."

Spirit Box — a male voice: "Where'd Dad go?"

Spirit Box — a male voice: "Start digging."

Paul thought he heard something. "What was that?"

Spirit Box — a male voice: "Nothing."

Spirit Box — a young male voice, very clear: "Help!"

Spirit Box — a male voice: "We need to … protect."

"What year is it?" I asked.

Spirit Box — a male voice: "I know, I know … I'll get him."

Spirit Box — a male voice: "Go get him!"

Spirit Box — a male voice: "I got him!"

Spirit Box — a male voice: "You didn't. Go dig!"

"Is there a reason you don't like us here?" I asked.

White noise.

"You want us to leave?" I asked.

Spirit Box — a male voice: "You bet."

Spirit Box — a male voice: "Get out!"

"Do you want us to stay?"

There was a mix of white noise and staccato static.

"I don't think I've ever heard that from the Spirit Box," Peter said.

"No," I confirmed.

"What's in the barn that's such a big secret?" Peter asked.

"What will we find in the barn?" Paul asked.

Spirit Box — a male voice: "We have … to go …"

Spirit Box — a male voice: "Clean!"

Spirit Box — a male voice: "We will."

Spirit Box — a male voice: "Clear!"

Spirit Box — a young male voice: "Bring Paul."

"Paul?" Peter asked.

"Yeah!" Paul said.

Spirit Box — a male voice: "He'll bring …"

Spirit Box — a male voice: "He'll bring it."

"May I ask you something? If we dig in the cellar of the barn, will we find bodies of people?" Peter asked.

Spirit Box — a male voice: "You'll get hurt."

Spirit Box — a male voice: "Burn!"

Spirit Box — a male voice: "Poison …"

Spirit Box — a male voice: "You know what? It ain't cruel."

Spirit Box — a male voice: "But father!"

Spirit Box — a young male voice with a Spanish accent: "Go, beat it home."

Spirit Box — a young male voice: "Okay."

"What's your last name?" Paul asked.

Spirit Box — a male voice: "Go piss off!"

"Give us your last name, please?" Paul asked again.

Spirit Box — a male voice: "Miriam."

Spirit Box — a female voice: "Your name."

Spirit Box — a male voice: "McGuinness, Malcom."

Spirit Box — a young male voice: "Wake up! Protect … the baby!"

Spirit Box — a female voice: "What happened?"

Spirit Box — a male voice: "The baby …"

Spirit Box — a male voice: "Elsbeth …"

Spirit Box — a male voice: "Found it!"

Spirit Box — a male voice: "What baby?"

Spirit Box — a male voice: "Corpse!"

Spirit Box — a male voice: "What if …"

Spirit Box — a male voice: "What if … I did?"

All of a sudden all communication stopped and after a few minutes of nothing but white noise I shut off the Spirit Box and we took a short break.

"What's that smell?" Paul said.

"Smells like urine, like stale urine," Peter replied.

"I don't smell anything.… Oh, yeah, I smell it," Victoria said.

I moved in closer and the smell seemed to move around the room, then it was gone.

"Let's go again," Peter said, turning his Spirit Box on.

Even before Peter had a chance to start questioning, a female voice said, "Can we talk?"

"Hello?" Peter asked.

Spirit Box — a female voice: "I must … had you."

Spirit Box — a male voice: "Oh!"

"What's my name?" Peter asked.

Spirit Box — a male voice: "I give up. Where were you?"

Spirit Box — a male voice: "The loft!"

"Who are you?" Peter asked.

Spirit Box —a female voice: "Josie! Aunt Esther!"

Spirit Box — a female voice: "Dave?"

Spirit Box — a male voice: "Wait!"

Spirit Box — a male voice: "Something's going on."

Spirit Box — a male voice: "Yeah, I know."

"Is there a Reverend here in the room?"

Spirit Box — a male voice with an accent: "Were you up … a hill?"

Spirit Box — a male voice: "Innocent!"

Spirit Box — a male voice, sounding panicked: "Help us!"

Spirit Box — a male voice: "Behind you. Hands off!"

"Is this sound making you crazy?" Peter asked.

Spirit Box — a male voice: "You little shit!"

Spirit Box — a male voice: "Be careful!"

Spirit Box — a male voice: "I'm begging to make it fit."

Spirit Box — a male voice: "Oh, I see it. It's got them all freaked out."

"Now, could someone speak to us, please?" Peter asked.

There was white noise.

"Is there a little girl up here?" Peter asked.

Again, white noise.

"Please don't be afraid."

White noise.

"We just want to talk."

White noise.

I was sitting on the floor and all of a sudden I felt it move beneath me. "You feel the floor moving?"

"Yeah, a little bit," Victoria said.

"Is somebody moving the floor, here?" Peter asked.

Spirit Box — a male voice: "Go … sing … bitch."

"Who are you?" Peter asked.

Spirit Box — a female voice:"Here I am … Laila."

Nothing but white noise.

"Peter, can you walk past us and head to the back so I can see how the floor reacts to you walking on it?" I asked.

Peter walked past and the floor vibrated. I felt the boards flex. "That seems pretty close to what I experienced."

"I didn't feel anything that way," Paul said.

"Except no one was walking then," Peter said.

"Where do you think he was going? This way or the other way?" Paul asked.

I shook my head. "I don't know."

Spirit Box — a male voice: "What do you know?"

"But it happened a few times, so he's either pacing or he's got a bunch of friends with him."

"I want to speak to the Reverend!" Peter said.

Spirit Box — a male voice: "Holler, if you can."

"Reverend Thompson, are you here?" Peter asked.

Spirit Box — a male voice: "I'm not talking."

"Why shouldn't we go back to the barn?"

Spirit Box — a female voice: "Whatever."

Spirit Box — a male voice: "Put it away."

Spirit Box — a male voice: "PLAY DEAD!"

Spirit Box — a male voice: "Can you help … mister?"

"Would you like to hear some music?"

Spirit Box — a female voice: "Play the … music … awesome!"

"You know you have nothing to fear from us. We've been here a dozen times. We've never hurt you before," I said.

Spirit Box — a male voice: "Play well."

Spirit Box — a male voice, gruff: "Play!"

Spirit Box — a female voice: "I'd like that."

"Are you afraid we'll send you somewhere you don't want to go?" Peter asked.

Spirit Box — a female voice: "We don't know."

Spirit Box — a female voice: "Help me?"

"Hm, it's just gibberish," Peter stated.

"I know," I said.

"I don't know; it's like hit-and-miss."

Peter turned the Spirit Box off.

Peter turned on a pre-made CD with period music and let the music filter throughout the rooms.

Peter started to search for Laila and Isabella, calling out their names. Paul and I walked over to the northwest room and I started asking for Miriam.

Other than the music, it seemed quiet. We asked questions for a few more minutes, then I instructed the team: "Let's head out to the barn."

As we headed to the kitchen to get our winter jackets, Paul stumbled backwards and recovered without falling.

"What did you just trip over, just now?" Victoria asked.

"I don't know. Man, I thought I was falling."

"Yeah, it looked like it," Peter said.

"You looked like you tripped over a log!" Victoria added.

Paul regained his composure, and we made sure he was okay before heading out.

We entered the barn and immediately headed up to the loft. Paul and I started to dismantle the surveillance system to take it downstairs to set it up in the cellar.

The microphone was recording Peter and Victoria talking about names.

"Jack?" Victoria said.

[A male voice saying, "Jeff," is picked up. It is followed by very quick chatter, almost like children chanting. Many voices saying all together, "Who me, who me, me, who, who."]

The system was switched off.

Peter heard an odd sound and started searching for its source. He found a loose, rusty latch holding a small west-side door closed, being moved by the wind. Peter fastened it down.

Paul and I moved the system to the cellar and set up.

Peter attempted communication in the loft, asking questions with hints of provocation. He climbed the steps at the north end and took several pictures, noting many dust orbs appeared in his photos. Victoria joined him for a short time.

Once the system was recording I came up and took some photos on the main floor. I then walked under the loft hatch and called up to Peter and Victoria to invite them to the cellar to dig.

Paul was alone in the cellar. He picked up a shovel and plunged it into the ground.

[A male voice is captured by the surveillance system saying, "Don't."]

Paul moved a few more shovelfuls of earth when he heard someone shuffling on the stairs to the cellar. He paused, looking toward the stairs, but no one was there.

A few moments later we all came down to join Paul, who had already dug a three-foot-deep hole in the mound.

"The ground is all sand," Paul told us.

"Just sand, that's strange," I said.

"No dirt, no rocks, just sand."

"Well X marks the spot," Paul said.

"Yeah," Victoria said in agreement.

[Male voice captured on surveillance: "Don't do that."]

Paul moved locations and started to dig another hole. Peter headed back upstairs to get another shovel so he could help dig. As he returned with the shovel and crossed the threshold between the storage area and the stable area, he inadvertently cracked the crown of his head hard against the top of the door frame. This injury confused him as he had crossed this opening many times prior and never came close to banging his head on the top of the door frame.

As Paul was still digging I turned on the Spirit Box.

Peter arrived back in the cellar and asked, "Want him to stop digging?"

Spirit Box — a male voice: "Yes."

"You want him to stop?

Spirit Box — a male voice: "Stop."

"Did you say stop?" Peter asked.

The response was unclear.

"What will he find if he digs further?" Peter inquired.

Spirit Box — garbled and quick: "Dead one"

Only Peter heard it.

Victoria heard, "Potato." We all laughed at that point.

Paul had dug several holes across the cellar without finding anything.

"I could dig here all night, we're not getting anything," Paul said.

"Maybe it's deeper," I suggested.

"I'm going down three feet," Paul said.

"Funny it's just sand," I said.

"Maybe they filled this cellar in with sand and it used to be deeper," Paul said.

I walked over and looked at the stair construction. "I don't think so, the way the frame for the stairs is made, they end right where they should for this floor depth."

Both Peter and Paul started to fill in the holes.

[The iris on the camera blurs and tries to focus, however nothing appears to be in its view.]

Peter played some music in the barn from his CD player.

"You guys can sing along," Peter said.

[The microphone captures a male voice: "Damn you!"]

The team moved up the stairs and was standing on the main floor, listening.

"It's just like a perfect night in the barn. Nothing like before," Paul said.

["Nothing," comes a male voice on the microphone.]

"I heard a voice," Victoria reported.

The team allowed the surveillance system to do its work as we listened to the music drifting up through the floor.

After about twenty minutes I suggested we head back to the cottage.

[The microphone detects rustling near the camera and what sounds like a door creaking open.]

We packed up our equipment and hauled it back to the cottage. I temporarily set up the surveillance system from the barn in the studio near the television as I wanted to attempt an ITC session later. Peter set up the CD player and started playing music.

As we were all standing in the studio talking, a sharp scent of stale urine trailed past us again.

[The second-floor surveillance system captures a female crying, possibly to the music playing.]

"Do you like the music?" Peter asked.

["Like the music," comes a female voice.]

As we approached the top of the stairs everyone paused; we could smell coffee brewing.

Peter shut off the music.

[There is a male voice calling, "Miriam."]

After exploring the house for the next twenty minutes, Paul and I headed outside for a break. Almost immediately, Paul spotted movement between a tree and a work van near the road side of the barn. One solid black shadow walked by the van and one white shadow passed further back beside Victoria's car. They appeared and then disappeared quickly.

"Crap! Did you see that?" Paul yelled out.

"That!" I replied, seeing only one of them at the end of the barn near the car. I quickly turned and ran to the back door of the cottage and called into the house for the team to bring flashlights and cameras. Immediately they joined Paul and me outside.

"We heard a noise and the shadowy one was just standing there watching us, that's when the other one appeared down further by Victoria's car, it was that one that sent the chills through me!" Paul explained.

The four of us walked down to where they had been and checked the vehicles and around the side of the barn. Scanning the area thoroughly we found nothing. As we walked slowly back from the barn, Paul told Victoria to take some pictures of the lit windows of the cottage. Victoria took the first picture and had a distinct feeling that someone was approaching her from behind. She felt the presence was approximately four to six feet away. She turned and looked over her right shoulder but saw nothing. As she raised her camera and took the second picture, she clearly felt a presence right behind her, looking over her shoulder. She snapped around quickly but didn't see anyone. Unnerved, she quickly walked away and was happy to see Paul was several feet in front of her. She explained later that the feeling was very real and she swore someone was in her personal space. This was the first time during the investigation here that she felt very uncomfortable and did not want to be on her own.

[Inside the cottage, the main floor camera picks up a yellowish orb crossing the living room heading directly for the kitchen. It turns 45 degrees in mid-flight and goes upstairs.]

Everyone came back into the cottage. Paul and I moved into the studio while Peter and Victoria remained in the kitchen, talking.

[The camera's microphone captures a female voice saying, "Get out."]

I moved to the main-floor surveillance system and started preparing for the ITC session. Victoria came in and sat down just as a male voice said, "Hey."

Victoria turned and looked up to acknowledge the voice, but then she realized it wasn't any one of us.

I finally got a dead channel on the television with nothing but white noise and snow and began filming. After a couple of minutes, there was a voice in the static that said, "Peter."

"We are researching the church," Peter said.

A male voice came back with, "I don't care."

There were undistinguishable whispers.

"Was it Alexander who decided the church should be moved here?" Peter asked.

"Yeah."

"Why did they have to move this house to this location from its original property? Did it have something to do with John's first wife?" I asked.

"No."

The roving stench of urine returned, catching Peter and Victoria's attention. They alerted us to it and we smelled it, too.

Communication via the television seemed to have gone quiet.

The urine smell returned with a vengeance.

"There's got to be something dirty in here," Paul stated, coughing.

I stopped the ITC session and turned the television off. I turned the surveillance camera back toward the studio, stairs, and kitchen doorway.

The team moved upstairs. As we arrived on the landing I noticed Victoria reacting to something. "What was that?" I inquired.

"I don't know. I thought I was hearing something," she reported.

"What'd you hear?" Paul asked.

"I thought I heard some chattering. I thought you turned on like a ... Did you hear it?" Victoria said.

"Yeah," I replied.

"Yeah, it was like, chattering. You heard it?" Paul said.

"What the heck was that?" Paul asked.

"I don't know. It sounded to me like a female, asking something," I told them.

Peter set up the CD player in the small bedroom at the top of the stairs to play some pre-recorded period music to try and illicit a response.

Peter left his recorder in the ensuite bathroom, the microphone pointed toward the open door and the bedroom beyond. He turned the lights off.

[Almost immediately there is a male voice shouting, "Hey!" Just as the first music track, "Rock of Ages," begins playing.]

[There is a definite thump/impact sound inside the bathroom during an instrumental version of "Silver Threads Among the Gold" captured on Peter's digital recorder.]

Peter turned the music off mid-song to test for any ghostly objections or reactions. There was a very faint pair of knocking sounds, but we were unable to determine where they originated from. Then there was a metallic-sounding impact coming from inside the bathroom.

I asked, "Do you want to hear more music? Can we play some more music for you? Are you enjoying the music?"

[Again there are a couple of light knocking sounds coming from inside the empty room. Then the same metallic sound, only much louder, coming from the bathroom.]

Paul, Victoria, and I moved out to the landing and settled around the open area. I took up a position on the top step.

"Hey, I smell coffee, like someone is making coffee," Paul reported.

Everyone acknowledged the scent of coffee. It lasted for a few moments then it vanished.

We attempted several minutes of communication without any positive results.

"Why don't we go outside and allow the recording systems to do their work?" Paul said.

With everyone in agreement we headed outside.

[There are more sounds partway through the beginning of the violin playing of the song "The Girl I Left Behind Me," then a loud footfall in the bathroom. There is a bang on the wall very close to a point of the song where the lyric would be punctuated.

There is a very loud movement sound in the same room as the recorder as someone bangs around downstairs in the kitchen.]

Victoria and I headed off to pick up coffee for the team. As I drove away I thought to myself, *Did the scent of coffee in the cottage subliminally inspire everyone to now want some?*

Peter and Paul re-entered the house. After asking several questions from inside the ensuite bathroom, Peter heard what he believed to be the sound of Paul coming up the stairs to join him. He picked the recorder up and headed to the stairs to find that Paul was still on the main floor. Peter came down and asked Paul if he had come up.

"No, I was down here taking photos," Paul told him.

Peter moved to the top of the stairs, settled on the landing, and asked several more questions, trying to reach the abusive male spirit.

Unsuccessful, Peter retrieved the CD player and took it downstairs, where Victoria and I had returned from our coffee run. The team gathered in the kitchen to take a break. Peter related his experience with Carol and Bonnie. Victoria began a discussion on dreams, and commented on the "reality" of vivid dreams and related it to what we perceive as reality.

[There is an extremely loud two-second burst of static over the recorder.]

When Peter reviewed it later he felt that this was the loudest burst ever caught on the recorder so far. Could this be a listener inspired to comment on Victoria's logic?

The rest of the coffee break was made up of sharing dream experiences from Paul and Victoria. I shared some of Einstein's theories on time and space.

[A male voice is captured saying, "Yeah, well ..." The voice is followed by three short knocks.]

Paul was talking about Judgment Day. "You have to be judged. Didn't you read the Book?"

[A very faint male voice responds, "No."]

After a very sobering discussion regarding life purposes and why some of the team chose to remain paranormal investigators/researchers the team exited the cottage for the barn. Peter brought the CD player along.

[As the team walks toward the barn, there is a male voice that seems to say, "Hi there. Hi." Could this be the older white-haired farmer-person greeting us in passing?]

We all entered the barn and spread out, taking photos and conducting EVP sessions.

[There is the sound of a bell, like that of an old-time school bell or distant church bell, captured on the digital recorder.]

Peter headed down to the cellar alone and prepared to start the CD player while talking out loud, "Well, Ricky, I don't know if you're really down here...."

[There is a deep male voice that replies matter-of-factly, "Yes."]

Peter started the CD and rejoined the others on the ground floor.

Peter ran into Victoria and they joined Paul and myself examining possible prints in the powder trap laid down in the storage area. Peter commented that the shapes in the powder reminded him of chicken feet. Paul commented on the mouse-like prints he thought he saw in the powder.

Paul attempted to take a picture of the powder, then exclaimed that his camera had failed again. He needed replacement batteries. Both Peter and I offered him some of our batteries.

"What do you need?" Peter asked.

[A soft, young male voice exhales and says, "Aw man!"]

"Double A's," Paul replied.

[The young male voice responds with a "hmph."]

As another track played below (male singing "Silver Threads Among the Gold"), I commented, "All the ghosts from all over the neighbourhood might be here."

"Hey, come along!" Peter said.

Paul moved up into the loft, yelling down to Peter, "Turn up the music."

Peter obliged, heading back down to the cellar and turning the volume up, then joined Paul in the loft. I climbed up and joined them there, taking photos. Victoria explored the ground floor solo. After a few minutes, Victoria appeared at the loft ladder.

"You know what? It's like the perfect night in the barn. Nothing like before," Paul stated.

"Yeah." Peter said in agreement.

"There was so much happening!" Paul said with excitement.

"Did somebody just say, 'Nothing'?" Victoria asked, looking into the loft.

"Yeah, me," Paul stated.

"Oh, you said it again?" Victoria confirmed.

"Again? Did you hear it twice?" Paul asked.

"You said, 'Just like nothing,' and then I heard, 'Nothing' again," Victoria explained.

"I only said it once," Paul said.

"Did either of you say, 'Nothing'?" she asked.

Neither Peter nor I had said anything.

"Okay, I heard it twice. I heard Paul said, 'Okay, it's like nothing,' and then I heard 'Nothing' repeat right after," Victoria stated.

After some more unsuccessful photos and attempts at communication, the team prepared to head back to the cottage. Peter retrieved the CD player from the cellar.

But I stopped in my tracks as we were leaving when I smelled human excrement. The odour passed quickly, but for a moment I felt like I couldn't get out of the barn fast enough. We headed back and Paul broke from the group to get a garbage bag from my car so we could start cleaning up.

[A male voice saying, "Ghost!" is captured on Peter's digital recorder.]

We entered the house and prepared the television and camera for an ITC session. Paul stumbled again, but did not fall. Peter and Victoria noted that the loss of balance was unusual for him.

"Second time that happened!" Paul reported.

I started off by inviting any of the spirits that may be present to communicate through the use of our equipment.

"Isabella, are you here?" Peter asked.

[A male voice replies, "I am."]

I adjusted the volume on the television set so as not to overwhelm the camera microphone.

"We're writing a book about the history of the church," I said.

[A voice immediately says, "No." Then it whispers, "No, don't!"]

Peter snapped a photo of the studio and then asked, "Laila?"

[A female voice that sounds extremely faint, as if heard through a bad telephone connection, says, "Yes."]

After a seemingly unsuccessful communication session, the team agreed to start packing up for the night.

Peter locked and closed the door to the cottage after wishing the residents a "Happy Easter." Peter and I walked Victoria to her car, as she was nervous after Paul's figure-sightings near it, earlier. Victoria drove away, leaving Paul, Peter, and me alone to talk over the night's events.

Conclusions:

My Spirit Box session included mention of a baby's corpse toward the end of it; Peter's short Spirit Box session produced several names being called.

· The team smelled dry urine "spots" four times in the cottage (main floor) and coffee brewing once.
· Later I smelled feces briefly, outside the cottage.
· Paul's balance was off more than once in the cottage; Peter crowned himself hard in the barn. (Both Paul and Peter are considered provocateurs when to comes to communication with spirits.)
· Paul captured a pair of photos illustrating a moving black "wall" in the main floor studio.

TRACK LISTING of the CD used in this investigation:
1. Rock of Ages (1775) (Choir)
2. Rock of Ages (Piano)
3. Silver Threads Among the Gold (1873) (Sterling Trio)
4. Silver Threads Among the Gold (Piano, Violin)
5. Silver Threads Among the Gold (Elsie Baker)
6. The Last Rose of Summer (1813)
7. Ella Waltz (1848)
8. Footsteps of Angels (1848)
9. The May Queen (1848)
10. Long Long Ago (1843) (Barbara Maurel)
11. Long Long Ago (Violin, Piano)
12. Meet Me in Heaven (1854)
13. The Girl I Left Behind Me (1840s)
14. Fisher's Hornpipe (1830)
15. Merrily Merrily Rounds the Bark (1815)
16. Pop Goes the Weasel (1853)

11

SIXTH INVESTIGATION
MID-APRIL

Paul and I arrived and met up with Peter. Shortly after, Victoria and James arrived, and we all entered the cottage. We talked about past EVP captured, then everyone gathered around my laptop to examine some of Paul's photos from our last visit.

James felt the need to ask for protection for himself and the rest of us before we commenced our investigation. He felt there was a great deal more negative energy there than just Nathan.

As the team prepared to set up equipment, someone coughed and there was a thump from upstairs.

[It is followed by a male EVP whispering, "Harder!"]

"What was that bang?" I asked, but no one else had heard it. Paul and I moved upstairs to set up the second surveillance camera, followed by Victoria. Shortly after, James and Peter left the ground floor studio to us upstairs.

[There is an unidentifiable noise close to the recorder placed on the tall shelf outside the northwest room on the main floor; no one is on that level at this time.]

[Upstairs, Peter's digital recorder captures sinister-sounding laughter. This is followed by a squeak.]

Victoria walked through the upper landing on her way back downstairs to retrieve her camera. She took a few test shots and then returned upstairs to the master bedroom.

[Several small sounds of movement — taps, shuffling, and impacts — begin at random around the main floor studio. The sounds grow louder. There is a loud impact sound, like something is dropped onto a solid surface. More loud sounds follow.]

With the second-floor surveillance system now recording, the team descended to the main floor.

Peter pulled the trapdoor to the crawlspace open and climbed down to place his E. Probe there. James came to the opening, and looking down, said, "So what's down there?"

"It's fairly small down here," Peter said.

James moved down into the crawlspace to have a look around while the rest of us remained in the kitchen.

[The main floor camera detects a male voice saying, "Get down."]

Peter pointed out the corner around the water heater tank to James.

[There is a two-second burst of loud static on Peter's digital recorder.]

As James and Peter began to note a hole in the cement floor, Peter said, "Yeah, I never did bring a flashlight."

[There is more static recorded, faintly this time.]

[There is a creak on the stairs as if someone is standing on them, captured by James's digital recorder.]

After investigating what appeared to be a hole filled with sand, they decided to leave the crawlspace.

As they were leaving the crawlspace Peter stepped on the bottom stair, causing a very loud creaking noise. When Peter makes a noise he will say, "tag" and comment on whatever he had done to cause a noise so it is not confused with any spirit activity. Peter said, "Tag that," as they headed back up the stairs.

[A male voice says, "Tag."]

James admitted laughing out loud when he later reviewed the audio-digital file. It sounded like whatever entity was there was helping them to tag noises we had made or was perhaps poking fun at Peter.

Peter left his recorder on top of the water heater tank to retrieve his flashlight from the main floor. He returned and they conducted a short EVP session, but it became hard to hear anything as the furnace kicked on. Peter and James exited the cellar, but left the E. Probe.

Paul and Victoria were upstairs, and headed through the hallway to come down to the main floor.

[A voice is recorded saying "Ya Misota." Either a foreign language or its meaning is lost to us.]

Paul, Victoria, and I moved to the exterior of the cottage to take photos of the windows. James and Peter joined us and suggested we visit the barn.

Paul was the first one in and headed directly up to the loft, taking pictures. Peter climbed into the loft and Paul reported raccoon tracks on the loft powder trap. James joined them shortly thereafter, and tried to take several photos, but reported that the camera could not seem to focus on anything.

[James's digital recorder captures a male voice calling his name, "James."]

Peter moved to the south end of the loft and reported feeling dizzy as he wandered the loft attempting communication.

Paul climbed down and joined Victoria and me on the ground floor.

James decided to leave the loft. Peter returned to the north side, laying the recorder on the third step from the top of the staircase. Peter tried a pendulum session. After several questions and no results, Peter noted the pendulum shaking/wobbling in place. He stopped the session. Paul, James, and I stepped out of the barn to investigate a very loud bang coming from outside.

Peter came down and Victoria headed up to the loft.

Peter wandered into the storage area to attempt communication; Victoria was also conducting an EVP session.

We all noticed a group of people quite a distance away on the next property having a BBQ and entertaining the children with a few fireworks, which explained the bang we had heard. We headed back into the barn.

Peter and James climbed down into the cellar to take photos. Peter spoke aloud: "If you heard me upstairs, you'll know what I said earlier about us coming back, and we're going to dig in more places and we're going to find your secret."

There was no reply.

Everyone met on the main floor and the team headed back to the cottage. Paul entered first.

[A male voice is captured on the camera microphone saying, "Damn you."]

Peter was the last into the cottage.

[Peter's digital recorder captures an EVP of a male saying, "Hey there, prick!"]

Victoria reported smelling urine again, but no one else picked up on it.

As Paul finished describing the door hinge story from a few visits back, James reported smelling the urine odour from inside the northeast room.

Soon after, Peter reported feeling a dull pain over his right knee as he stood at the north end of the studio.

I pointed out that a lot of strange things seemed to be happening; between similar pains in our legs, feeling dizzy and disoriented, and tripping over non-existent things. We needed to be careful.

We decided to head out for lunch and allow the surveillance systems to do their work.

Peter placed the recorder inside the stairwell alcove on top of some upright objects and closed the door, completely securing the latch on the door.

Everyone left the house and immediately activity began, captured on Peter's digital recorder and both the surveillance system microphones:

Light, bounce-like movement outside the closet, followed by a scratch/flick sound near the recorder inside the closet.

A tick sound outside the closet loud enough to be heard from inside the closet. Slight movement/click sound, likely outside the closet. A particularly loud flick sound, sounding like the latch of the closet door. There is a dull thud outside the closet (possibly a footfall?) Then the unthinkable, a sharp, loud knock raps on the closet door.

Suddenly, the sound "dips" three times as something affects the recorder microphone.

A faint click sound, from deeper inside the closet. Again the sound cuts out, this time twice. A dull impact sound — possibly inside the closet, but could be on the overhead stairs.

Noises resembling a piece of paper being rapped on outside the closet, and a very distinct impact sound inside the closet and a soft slap, like flesh on a solid surface.

The main floor surveillance camera microphone also picked up activity:

A male saying, "get back." There are two bangs originating from the studio and the camera is bumped, causing the image to slide right a few inches.

On the upper floor there is a male speaking an unknown language, the sound of a door closing, rustling material near the camera, and a female voice saying, "They are not going away yet."

The second-floor camera microphone goes quiet for a long period of time and then records two males laughing.

The team returned and entered the cottage; Peter opened the closet and retrieved his digital recorder.

Paul and I checked the surveillance systems to ensure everything was working correctly. Paul noticed the camera was pointing slightly off from the direction it was originally set up and shifted the camera back to the correct position.

Paul headed downstairs, but I was still bothered by the camera being moved and stood quietly near the bedroom door. After a few moments, I turned to leave and the floor creaked behind me near the bathroom. I returned to the spot to see if I had possibly made the sound, and that's when I heard what sounded like a huff, a deep exhale of frustration coming from the door to the bathroom.

I heard it there, hiding in the shadows, something that had been long dead. My first thought was to run. But there would be no running, as this encounter was why I had come to this place — to meet and speak with the dead.

Standing my ground, I turned to face the bathroom and asked, "Who's there?" followed by, "What is your name?"

I gave it a minute or two, not knowing if there would be a response. I stepped in closer and looked into the bathroom, half expecting to see something. Nothing was there, and after a long pause I turned and went downstairs. Upon later review of the surveillance equipment, there was no response recorded.

Peter and I discussed heading over to interview a previous owner of the property to see if we could get any more background information. I sent the team off to investigate the barn as we prepared to leave.

[Upstairs, the camera microphone records a male calling, "Emma."

"Stop it," says a male voice.

Unintelligible words.

A long pause.

"Bring it downstairs," the male says. There are a couple of footsteps.

"I'll thrash them!" an older male says.

"Yeah," a younger male replies.]

I exited the cottage with the rest of the team as they headed off to the barn, but waited for Peter. Peter noticed the distinct odour of manure and straw as he exited the washroom and entered the studio. The patch of odour disappeared quickly. He came out and joined me in the driveway and we walked to the previous owner's house. Peter and I were greeted by a relative of the previous owner and were told that she was away until the following week. We thanked her and returned to the property, going directly to the barn to join the rest of the team. We spent about a half hour taking photos and examining every inch of the barn, but for some reason this visit to the barn seemed extremely quiet.

Peter entered the cottage alone and said aloud, "I'm alone in the world." He headed to the studio.

[The main floor surveillance microphone picks up a male voice agreeing with him saying, "Yeah."]

The rest of us entered the cottage and went into the studio.

[The main floor surveillance camera microphone captures a male voice telling us to "Get out!"]

We shared some of the information found from the surveillance analysis from our previous visit with the rest of the team. We started to talk about the tenants who rented the place. I said, "What was it, the 70s?"

[A voice says, "Se —" and a deep exhale.]

As Peter described the previous "professional tenants" who left "in the middle of the night" without paying back-owing rent, there is a burst of static on his digital recorder.

After about an hour of trying to communicate in the cottage, everyone decided to go back to the barn do some more digging.

Peter stopped at his car to grab two shovels and set down his digital recorder.

[It captures a low-pitched male voice growling something indistinguishable. "Here is that _____ to whack."]

Paul and I went into the cellar and inspected the floor, trying to decide where we should dig next.

Peter dropped the shovels at the door and climbed up into the barn loft, sweeping the barn for EMF spikes using a gauss meter. Victoria and James inspected the main floor. Paul and I made our way into the loft and discovered our cameras and flashlights were being drained of power. James and Victoria arrived in the loft.

James reported feeling pain in his left leg. Shortly afterward I experienced pain in my left leg as well. It was not the first time I'd had this pain, as I had experienced it on a previous visit to the property.

Peter performed a pendulum session; the agate pendulum shivered without turning or swinging in response to the team's questions. After no responses, Paul suggested a "squeeze" (where the team splits up to inhabit each room of a building and ask questions, hoping to capture EVP. The placement of a team member in each area will not allow the spirit anywhere to go, essentially forcing a face-to-face confrontation). He exited the loft with Victoria and James, leaving Peter and me to try a Spirit Box session in the loft.

As Peter asked questions from the north end of the barn, I took photos. I noticed that there seemed to be a wall of darkness that had appeared where previously my flash had brightened the entire north wall. Now there was a very black barrier between me and that wall.

After several minutes of asking questions and receiving no responses, I activated the Spirit Box (FM reverse at 100 milliseconds). Five minutes elapsed with no responses.

Peter proposed starting a new recording of a Spirit Box session, this time locked onto white noise, solely with the intent of playing the recording back at a slower speed to possibly allow us to hear any responses cleaner and without background sounds.

As the pure, white-noise Spirit Box session started, I noted for the recorder that the box was "locked at 85.5 megahertz."

Peter asked, "Is there someone in the hayloft?" There were loud static bursts from the Spirit Box. All seemed to go quiet again and after asking a few dozen questions over the white noise we received no responses at all.

"Are your photos still showing that darkness?" Peter asked.

"No, bright as day," I told him.

We determined we were alone in the loft and deactivated the Spirit Box.

Paul dug another hole in the cellar without finding anything. He gave up as there was very little space to dig new holes. Paul, James, and Victoria came up to the main floor and Peter and I climbed down from the loft. The team exited the barn and walked back to the cottage. It was snowing heavily. Peter and I hung back and conversed under the garage eave. I noticed that the Spirit Box had been turned on; I pulled it from my pocket. "This was shut off when we were done in the loft."

"Could it just turn back on?" Peter asked.

"No, you have to push and hold the power button, and you also have to slide the switch on for the speaker," I explained.

James was already inside the cottage looking at some of the artwork in the studio. Paul heard crackling sounds, which he thought were coming from upstairs. He headed up to investigate. Later we would discover that these sounds were coming from behind the main floor camera.

Peter set his E. Probe on a folding table in the middle of the studio.

I headed over and checked to ensure the surveillance system was operating properly and walked into a cloud of something in the middle of the room, which made me start to choke. It left an awful taste in my mouth, but had no smell.

Just then Victoria reported smelling urine again. Everyone started snapping photos of the area.

Peter and Victoria suggested a coffee run and the rest of us decided to go outside for some air. As James moved toward the kitchen he had to move between where I was standing and where the folding table was. Something unseen pushed between him and the table, knocking him into me and setting off Peter's E. Probe on the table. Paul was a few feet away and saw the entire incident. "Whoever that was wanted to get outside before we did," he said.

Everyone left the building.

"I'm telling you, they are watching us like a hawk, every time we go outside they follow us because they think we are going to the barn," Paul explained.

[The latches on Peter's equipment case start to click as if someone is flicking them open and closed.]

Peter and Victoria arrived with the coffee. After the break we decided to conduct a Spirit Box and pendulum session at the same time; our focus was to communicate with Isabella.

Peter proposed playing some period music upstairs in the smaller bedroom. Peter started the music beginning with the choir singing "Rock of Ages," and returned to the main floor studio.

[Immediately there is audio activity upstairs being captured on the surveillance microphone.

Male voice: "Want them to set us free."

Female voice: "Free."]

I set the SB-7 Spirit Box to sweep FM frequencies in reverse at 100 milliseconds.

Even before we started the session there was a soft voice coming over the speaker saying, "Hello."

Peter responded: "Hello."

Spirit Box: "What the ..."

Peter: "What the?"

Peter: "Remember us?"

Spirit Box: "Don't think so."

While no one spoke, there was a soft thud that came from the upstairs, estimated to originate from the bathroom, as the male vocal version of "Silver Threads Among the Gold" was playing. "Did you hear that sound, something moved?" I asked.

The team agreed, they all had heard the noise.

There was a click and a thump sound from the second floor. Peter and I acknowledged hearing this as well.

Spirit Box — a female voice: "That's nice."

Spirit Box — a male voice: "Nice."

We believed they could be talking about the music.

Spirit Box — a male voice calls: "Carol."

There are the distinct sounds of walking.

Spirit Box — a female voice: "I can hear you."

Victoria reported smelling the urine again very briefly, as though it just passed by her. She was curious if the smell was coming from something in the room like the carpets, and after a closer examination she was sure it was.

I sneezed.

[The main floor camera records a female saying, "Bless you."

Then a male yells, "Turn it off!"]

"Isabella are you here?" Peter asked.

Spirit Box — a female voice: "Hello."

Peter: "Are you not Isabella?

Spirit Box: "Yes."

Peter: "Is this Alexander?"

Spirit Box: Undetermined response.

"Do you have anything you'd like to say to us?" Peter asked.

Spirit Box: "Sure." [Pause] "Help you."

All went quiet for a few moments, then from the Spirit Box over several frequencies a voice said, "Don't!" A moment later, "Watch the back ..."

It sounded like there was a female and a male who wanted to warn us of something but another male was telling them, "Don't!"

I decided to shut down the Spirit Box and just focus on the pendulum. I began the pendulum session, asking it to show me the direction for "Yes." The pendulum turned clockwise.

I asked it to show me the direction for "No."

[The digital recorder captures a faint voice saying, "No."]

The pendulum turned counter clockwise.

"Isabella, are you here?"

Pendulum: yes.

"Did you have a good relationship with your husband, John?"

Pendulum: no motion.

"Did John harm you in any way? Physically or mentally?"

Pendulum: no motion.

"Are you afraid to answer?"

Pendulum: no motion.

"Did he ever hurt your daughter?"

Pendulum: no motion.

"Are you buried with your family?"

Pendulum: no motion.

"John, are you here?"

Pendulum: no motion.

"John, are you silencing your wife from talking to us?"

Pendulum: no motion.

"We are all here as friends. Thank you."

As Peter attempted to start a pendulum session of his own, I determined that there seemed to be a strong presence that was holding communication back from willing spirits.

"Did any bootlegging take place on this property?" Peter asked.

Pendulum: no motion.

"Did anybody run rum or alcohol from this property? Be honest now, please."

Pendulum: no motion.

"Was the property used as a church at one time?" I asked.

Pendulum: no motion.

[The digital recorder captures a small female voice murmuring, "Hm-hm," in response.]

We observed Peter's pendulum quivering in place as it hung plumb.

"I've seen this before; it might indicate someone is being repressed by a stronger influence," I explained.

[Peter's digital recorder captures a disturbing EVP, several seconds of the sound of someone vomiting.]

[Victoria's digital recorder also captures someone retching and vomiting.]

I had a strategy for this type of situation and went on to explain it to the team. "In the case of complete hesitation or lack of communication due to a dominate spirit holding others silent, the investigators must set up two communication sessions simultaneously in the furthest points from each other within the dwelling. It is rare that the dominant spirit will be able to control both locations at the same time and therefore will have to choose a place to be, allowing the other team to be open for communication. I call this 'Divide and Conquer.'"

After a short discussion on the best way to proceed, Paul, James, and Peter headed out to the barn. Victoria and I remained in the cottage, on the main floor in the studio. I gave them a few minutes to get to the barn and started asking questions before I began our own pendulum session. If Paul was right and the aggressive ones did follow them out to the barn, then I would have little trouble establishing communication.

I began the pendulum session.

"Miriam, are you here? Miriam? Will you speak with me, please?" — I paused — "Is there someone who wishes to speak for Miriam?"

There was a very hesitant response from the pendulum.

"Is there anyone here who wishes to speak?"

Pendulum: no response.

"My friends are digging in the barn. Do you think they will find something there? Will they find something in the barn? Is that where you keep the secrets?"

Pendulum: no.

"Is there a secret?" Victoria asked.

Pendulum: no.

"What happened to John's wife? What happened to Isabella, John's wife? Did she die here? Was she sent away?" I asked.

The pendulum stayed neutral but strong.

"Wow, it wants to answer, but it's just going back and forth. I can feel it pulling, right here."

"Are you not allowed to tell us?" Victoria asked.

Pendulum: no.

"Is that the secret? Can you tell us if that's the secret?"

The pendulum remained neutral.

"This is very unusual. I'm trying to find out if a boy who wears glasses died on this property. Did a young boy die on this property?"

Pendulum: no response.

"Do you have anything to say to us?" I asked.

[The main floor camera microphone captures a deep male voice saying, "She left me."]

Days later I became aware of this EVP and had to wonder if this was John talking about his wife, Isabella.

"Not getting any answers," I said.

"Annie, are you here?" I changed strategy. "Annie, are you here? Miriam, are you surprised that we're all alive?"

Finally the pendulum sprang to life: no.

"Were you expecting visitors when we showed up?"

Pendulum: yes.

"Did we interrupt your visit?"

Pendulum: large yes.

"I want to apologize; we didn't mean to interrupt anything. [Pause] Are you from Scotland?"

Pendulum: no.

"Are you from Europe?"

Pendulum: yes.

"Are you Dutch?"

Pendulum: yes.

"Thank you. Did you know Isabella?"

Pendulum: yes.

"Thank you. Were you related to her?

Pendulum: no.

"Did you help to run the church?"

Pendulum: yes.

"Thank you."

"There was a boy that was killed on a bicycle not far from here. Did he come here? Did he come by, looking for help?"

Pendulum: no.

"Do you know which boy I mean?"

Pendulum: no.

"Maybe because he didn't come by," Victoria pointed out.

"Miriam, do you have children?" Victoria asked.

Pendulum: no response.

"Miriam, do you have children of your own?"

Pendulum: no response.

"Does this house still receive many visitors?"

Pendulum: yes.

"Do you like the music playing, upstairs? Do you want us to play more music?"

Pendulum: no.

"It's not really your cup of tea?" Victoria said.

"Do you want something more modern?"

Pendulum: strong no.

"Is there something in this house that should not be here?

Pendulum: yes.

"Do they cause you harm?"

Pendulum: yes.

"Do they go between here and the barn?"

Pendulum: yes.

"Are they here right now?" Victoria asked.

Pendulum: no.

"Have they gone to the barn?"

Pendulum: yes.

"Are they out at the barn, right now?"

Pendulum: yes.

"Do they appear as children?"

Pendulum: yes.

"They appear as children?"

Pendulum: yes.

"Yes," Victoria said.

"Yes. But they are not children."

Pendulum: strong no.

"Do they mean us harm?"

Pendulum: neutral.

"You don't know?"

"She wouldn't know their intentions. Thank you."

I turned to look at Victoria and exhaled. "Well, that's not good!"

"No," Victoria agreed.

"Not good at all." I resumed the session. "Is there more than one of these child-like things?"

Pendulum: yes.

"Is there more than two of them?"

Pendulum: yes.

"Is there more than three of them?"

Pendulum: yes.

"Is there five of them?"

Pendulum: no.

"Then there must be four of them?"

Pendulum: yes.

"Thank you."

"Do they smell of urine?" Victoria asked.

Pendulum: yes.

"Are they foul?"

Pendulum: large yes.

"Are they here with us now?"

Pendulum: no.

"Those guys better watch their asses."

I pulled my cell phone out of my pocket and dialed Paul's number but got an unavailable signal.

"So much for Plan A. I think we should go out there. Do you want to go?"

"Okay, yeah, I'm not staying here by myself! Not if I start smelling urine!"

Victoria and I donned our jackets and exited the cottage and headed to the barn.

I pulled the barn door open and we entered. "It's just us, guys. Guys?"

I felt a moment of nervousness when there was no reply.

"Hello?" I yelled out.

Peter, Paul, and James all heard footsteps above them.

The guys down in the cellar suddenly stopped what they were doing. They could hear the sound of someone upstairs, not knowing it was Victoria and I. They froze and looked at each other, wondering what the hell was going on above them.

They were instantly relieved when they heard Victoria calling out.

"Hello?" Peter's voice called up from the cellar.

"It's just us," Victoria said.

Everyone climbed up to the main floor and I brought them up to speed on what I was getting back in the cottage. As Victoria entered the cellar, James picked up on her worried expression. "What's the matter?" He asked.

"Oh, we were just doing a pendulum session, and it was saying that there's some not-so-good … little things … like …"

"What?" James asked.

"It opened up the communications once you guys started this, so I decided to ask about those little grey things. And I asked, 'Is there something in the house that's not good?' and I got an indication of 'Yes.' I asked, 'Do they appear as children?' I got a 'Yes.'"

"He asked, "Are they children? And got a 'No' reply," Victoria stated.

"But I also asked 'Are they children?' And it said 'No.' 'Do they cause harm?' And it said 'Yes.' So when I asked 'Are they here, now?' And it said 'No.' I figured they must've left. It gave me an indication there's four of them, which is interesting because that's what the other medium said."

"Yeah, she said at least two in the house at the time and two or three down here," Peter added.

"And I asked if they smelled of urine and it indicated 'Yes,'" Victoria said.

"And I asked, are they foul? The answer was 'Yes.' So I wanted to come and see if you guys were getting anything out here."

"So he called you!" Victoria told Paul.

"I called your phone; it's out of service."

Paul checked his phone: no service.

"Yeah, it's dead down here. I checked my phone too and got nothing," James said.

Peter related what had happened with the pendulum and digging in the cellar. Paul expressed his doubts about anything buried in the cellar. Peter continued digging away at the hole he had started.

Victoria headed down to the cellar alone. "Do you remember me? Can you bang on something?" Victoria asked.

Immediately there was a knock. It was loud and sounded very close to her.

"Is that you knocking? Can you knock again?"

There was second knock, this time sounding distant and faint.

We all climbed down to the cellar and joined Victoria. Paul started digging again.

"Please, we need your help. Use my energy to direct this pendulum," Peter pleaded.

[There is the longest burst of static recorded to date. It sounds varied and breaks its regular rhythm partway through.]

"Okay, this is what we're going to do …" Paul began. He suggested he move from place to place so that Peter could ask the pendulum if he should dig wherever the pendulum indicated.

Peter asked if Paul should dig under where the cat's body used to be. The pendulum started shaking, vibrating noticeably.

"Is there something here that's bigger than you? Something scaring you?" Peter asked. There was a wooden thump from outside the cellar, followed by a pair of soft footfalls on cement.

"I just heard footsteps upstairs," James reported.

Without receiving any further "word" from the pendulum, Paul decided to start digging.

As Peter asked, "Should Paul stop?" a light static joined his voice.

"Is Paul digging in the right spot?" Peter asked.

Paul dug deeper, rapidly hacking away.

[As Paul digs into the sand, a higher-pitched buzz of static is recorded. But it is difficult to assess when this sound ends, as a loud scrape from the shovel blocks all other noises.]

Paul stopped, then resumed digging as Peter continued using the pendulum.

"Is that a 'yes'? Is he doing the right thing by digging there?" Peter asked. "Is he close?"

The pendulum was wobbling all over the place. There was an indication of a small 'yes,' growing stronger.

"Is he getting closer … to finding a secret?"

Paul asked for a flashlight to illuminate the hole he'd dug.

Pendulum: larger yes.

"Is there a body buried under the sand somewhere?"

Pendulum: yes.

"How far should he go down? Three feet?"

Pendulum: yes, getting larger.

"Four feet?"

Pendulum: yes

"More than four feet?"

Pendulum: yes.

"More than four feet? What is he, joking?" Paul said.

"Are you getting excited about this?"

Pendulum: large yes and growing.

"Are you getting anxious?"

Pendulum: yes.

"Is there somebody with us who doesn't want this to happen?"

Pendulum: growing yes.

"Well, tough noogies, 'cause it's happening."

Pendulum: growing yes. Now circling the area of Peter's open palm.

After Paul reported he'd dug at least two feet down, he said, "I don't see any bones." *[This is followed by some more light static.]*

"Should he dig farther than that?"

Pendulum: yes.

"Are you lying?" Peter asked, "Are you just lying to us? There's nothing where he's digging?"

Pendulum: slows down.

"Probably two-and-a-half feet, buddy … and there's nothing," Paul reported.

"Well, it did say four feet."

"Yeah, well, you're not going to get four feet," Paul said.

Peter started digging a different hole; Paul started a new one as well and instructed James to take random shots of the staircase periodically.

James confirmed the time: 11:30 p.m. The team began to wonder where the time went to and shared a laugh over "missing time."

Paul, James, and I headed up to the main floor.

Peter continued digging for a short time while Victoria watched, then resigned himself to filling the hole back in again.

Smoothing out the surface of the floor with a small piece of wood, Peter mischievously drew the sign of the cross on the area he was digging and joked it might garner a shocked reaction from anyone who entered the cellar.

Peter and Victoria came up and joined the rest of us.

James and I heard what sounded like two men whispering near the side of the barn, and headed off to investigate, leaving Paul and Victoria to watch the door and field at the side of the barn.

Peter exited the barn and joined Paul and Victoria outside.

"James and Richard had heard some voices around the barn," Victoria reported.

Nothing was found so we headed back, disappointed.

"Anything?" Paul asked, shining his flashlight at us.

"No."

"What'd you hear? A male?" Paul asked.

"Sounded like two, just whispering."

The team headed back inside the cottage. Peter and I entered last, closing the door behind us.

In the empty cottage the main floor surveillance camera microphone recorded activity.

["Mrs. Robinson," comes a male voice.

Male voice: "Harry, who's that?"]

We stopped to compare notes concerning the chain of recent events.

Peter then opened the trapdoor to the cottage crawlspace to retrieve the E. Probe and commented on the warmth of the bottom of the trap door itself plus the heat coming from the crawlspace area. He started descending and commented on the smell of mothballs/camphor. He tested the E. Probe, turned it off, and exited the crawlspace, closing the trap door and re-positioning the thin rug over it.

Victoria was ready to leave, so Peter and I walked her to her car. The recorder was left in the studio to listen as Paul and James packed up equipment and swept the floor.

As they worked inside James had his digital recorder operating.

[James's recorder detects first a woman's voice saying something we can not determine and then a child's laughter.]

The cars were packed and the house was secured and we all departed.

Conclusions:

- This investigation marked the first overt amount of malicious, aggressive, threatening phenomena on the property.
- Sinister-sounding laughter in the main floor studio area of the cottage was recorded twenty-four minutes into the investigation.
- James's sense of a foul-mouthed spirit's response to Peter's probing questions in the barn cellar; general threats were made to Peter this night, including sinister chuckling recorded in the cottage loft later.
- Dried urine smell was detected no less than three times on the main floor of the cottage; Peter smelled a manure-and-straw odour when he was alone in the studio at one point.
- Peter experienced dull pain over his right knee for about ninety seconds while standing still in the studio area of the cottage.
- My photos of a black "wall," limiting the camera flash's reach toward the straw-filled area, where Peter was standing.
- My coughing and tasting "something awful" at one point in the barn.
- First signs of communication repression during pendulum sessions.

12

THE VISITATIONS

Peter's House

At 12:20 in the morning Peter was heading toward his bedroom, when ahead of him in the hall there was a sudden shift on the floor between the bathroom and spare bedroom. The sound was as if someone were standing there and his approach had startled them into launching themselves away toward the spare room, casting a dark shadow as it moved. The incident caused him to pause.

Later that morning he woke to the sound of the alarm clock, but it felt like he had hardly slept. Peter made his way to the kitchen and started to prepare lunch for his daughter to take to school. It was at that point he noticed the clock on the wall read 3:48 a.m. He put everything away and headed back to bed where he confirmed his alarm clock was set for 5:55 a.m.

Paul's House

It was late, 2:30 in the morning, when the sound of scratching from a few feet away in the closet door woke Paul from sleep. He rose, turning on the light and looking to the door. The scratching got louder, the sound of human nails being dragged across the wood about midway up the door.

He walked to the door and felt an unmistakable cold electrical tingling. He pulled the door open and nothing was there. He retreated from the cold he was feeling, still watching the door as the sound persisted. Then all at once it stopped and the room immediately felt warmer.

My House

It was early Friday evening, about twenty hours prior to our investigation at the cottage, when there was a sound on the floor just inside our patio door. My wife, our dog, and I were watching television in the living room when we heard the sound of something shuffling on the floor. We both felt a heavy feeling come over us and there seemed to be an electrical charge in the air. As we looked at each other, our dog began to snarl and took off to the border of the room. The electrical energy and a foreboding seemed to fill the room, and the dog spun around and looked at its hindquarters as if something was nipping at them. He quickly ran, jumped up on the couch, and sought refuge beside my wife.

The dog started to react as if something was poking at him and my wife covered his side with her arm. I got up and yelled, "Leave my dog alone!"

I had a sense that whatever this was had a male energy feel to it.

Growling, the dog strained to look down the hall toward the kitchen. I walked into the kitchen and felt it there, the feeling was extremely heavy, almost sickening. I called to my wife to let her know it was now in the kitchen then returned to the living room. We tried to ignore it and proceeded to watch our television show. Soon after, the feeling dissipated and then it was gone altogether. I believe the message was clear: "If you come to my house and mess around, then I will come to yours." These are the risks of doing what we do.

As if this wasn't unnerving enough, there is a very important side story here.

My wife and I bought this house at the end of November 2012. It wasn't long after that we came to realize that our house had a resident spirit living in it, nothing bad, and the consensus between my wife and I was that it was that of a child. It seemed curious to know what we were doing in the house and our dog felt very comfortable around it, making visits to one of our spare bedrooms each morning and each night just prior to bedtime. What was disturbing to us was that after this visit from whatever it was from the cottage, we noticed over the next few months that our resident spirit was no longer there. Did it go freely, or was it forcibly taken? Questions I am sure I will never know the answers to.

James's House

James relayed an incident where he had left for work and his wife was in the shower. Moments later, his wife sensed someone near the bathroom door. She felt it was James, but was unnerved enough to get out of the shower and check the entire house. She found no one.

Victoria's House

Most disturbing of all reports coming from the team was Victoria telling us of her children's encounters with shadow people — one wearing a hat — and how even the family dog was noticing things moving in the upstairs hallway of her home.

13

SEVENTH INVESTIGATION
LATE APRIL

Peter and I arrived at the cottage property on a bright, sunny, breezy late-April afternoon and met the owner at the cottage at 3:00 p.m. Digging of the foundation of the owners' future home had obviously begun, as the adjacent field sported a house-sized crater surrounded by mountains of freshly unearthed soil and abandoned digging equipment. Though we had an appointment to meet a previous owner across the road to gather some historical data, we did some catching-up and I presented the owner with a report describing highlights of The Searcher Group's findings at the cottage and the barn to date. Before she and her husband left the property for the evening, the owner revealed that two days earlier, she brought her pet cat to the property and had intended to return home with it, but it bolted from her car before she could stop it and now the cat was missing. We vowed to watch out for her pet, said goodbye, then walked across the street to the home of previous owner.

We met with her as she stepped out onto her porch to join us. We explained why we had contacted her, and that we were looking for information about her old property across the road. She began by describing the size of the original property, which had extended all the way to a nearby cemetery. I couldn't put the size of the property into acres, but as a city kid, it would have to be ten city blocks, easy.

She went inside and came back with an old photo album and showed us pictures of the shed and barn at the back of the property and of an older gentleman standing with his horse.

She went on to describe that the property had been a working farm, and that asparagus, corn, and strawberries were grown there.

Peter showed her the picture of Barn Boy and immediately she denied recognizing him.

She did suggest that Barn Boy may be somewhere among her album of old pictures and referred to school pictures. Peter took the opportunity to ask after old township public school photos from the sixties.

She showed us a few of her school photos from 1945, and explained that she had been driving the school bus for forty years.

Peter informed her that the focus of the research at the property was on spirits and she became immediately intrigued. She said, "I know the boys used to call it the Spook Room upstairs, because it was dingy and it had three rooms up there. I think it was just because it was dark and they'd see the shadows of the cars going by."

Returning to the subject of ghosts, she said, "No, I never heard them say anything like that. They never talked about the place at all."

"I wonder if I should speak with your brother?" Peter asked

"He doesn't know anything, 'cause I called him. All he knows is what's on that paper."

"Well, if we mentioned ghosts, do you think, if his mind went there, he'd be like, 'Oh, if that's why you wanted to know'? Then maybe …"

"Well, he said he didn't know anything, 'cause I asked him to come down and he said, 'I don't know anything!' So I went, 'Okay.'"

"So I guess if there was an accident or an unexpected death or something, he would know that."

"Nobody's said anything. But you never know, I mean, there could be."

"Would you mind if I contacted him, then?"

"No, go right ahead!"

"Do you have his number handy by any chance?"

"No I don't. I don't know his number; I don't phone him very much. He lives in Georgetown."

This was an odd comment to make, since she just finished saying she'd been in touch with him recently.

"But he's never said anything about ghosts, so I don't ..." she added.

There was a pause in the conversation as we looked at some of the old photos.

She then continued, confessing she was interested in ghosts herself. She asked after our group's progress and when Peter revealed it was quite "busy," she said, "Oh, now I'm interested!" with a laugh.

She sounded very intrigued when Peter revealed that a "relic" was found behind the walls of the former shed. (Meaning the pistol.)

It was revealed her daughter lived for a time on the property looking after Laila (one of the previous inhabitants of the cottage, who we had been in contact with), but that she'd never shared any paranormal experiences while she lived there. She also told us that her daughter used to live in the white building below the cemetery and that while she was there, "things were happening" and that apparently that the complex used to house bodies awaiting burial over winter months. She explained that her daughter would likely have told her about anything ghostly, because she knew Elsie was interested in that kind of thing, too.

We thanked her for her time and for the collection of photocopied photos and headed back to the cottage. Peter and I left her with our Searcher Group contact cards.

Peter left his digital recorder in the cottage on the table in front of the northwest room and exited the house. We drove into Georgetown South to pick up my wife, Michelle, who would be joining us on tonight's investigation, at the local coffee shop.

[As we drive away, the digital recorder picks up activity in the house. There is a pair of tapping sounds, then the clear intonations of an older male's voice sounding as if he is entering the house from the back door. The words are indistinguishable, but the impression is of someone tapping their shoes of mud just outside the open door as they speak to someone else.

There is a very small knock on wood somewhere near the recorder, in the studio area on the ground floor. There is a light-weight skittering sound that is caught skipping 4x past/near the recorder. This is followed by a small thump, then something crunchy-sounding as if someone is stepping through dry crackers on the floor near the recorder.]

Joan and James arrived and waited outside for our return.

Not long after, we all congregated outside and caught up for a few minutes.

[On the digital recorder there is a pair of wooden footfalls a distance from the recorder, possibly on the staircase, followed by a sliding sound.]

"Did we get much in the barn last time?" James asked.

"We got some great stuff," I told him.

[James's digital recorder captures a voice sounding shocked saying, "Really."]

Peter entered the cottage. He deposited a coffee in the kitchen, took another with him and exited, rejoining us outside for a while longer.

[There is a small tap or movement near the recorder and a male voice saying "Ghost."

Shortly after there is significant movement around the recorder — a loud, solid, crash or impact sound, like something slapping the table or nearby bookcase.]

We started to unpack the verhicle and bring the equipment inside. Peter re-entered the house with a camera system in a tote box, put it down, then left for more equipment.

[A male hiccup or sharp intake of breath is recorded.]

We all entered the cottage. As the team started to get settled in the studio, I set up the surveillance equipment.

[There is a loud snap sound, which is repeated, followed by a light, indistinguishable female whispering under James's voice.]

Joan picked up the photo of Annie and said, "We will see this one tonight, for sure."

Once I had the main floor surveillance system up and running, I moved to the second floor to set up a similar system in the master bedroom, facing down the hall toward the stairs.

Everything was operating correctly and I started to move along the hallway of the second floor.

[There is a male voice captured saying, "Yeah."]

As I headed downstairs to the main floor a high energy field near the camera caused it to buzz and the iris attempted to focus on something unseen.

[All goes quiet and for twenty-six minutes there is no activity until the microphone picks up heavy walking near the camera, and the camera is bumped.

Long pause.

Female voice: "John."

Male voice: "Are you John? Are you John?"

Female voice: "Where's John?"
Male voice: "Is that you thrashing?"
A young female voice:"No."
Male voice: "No."
Female voice: "That was me."
Long pause.
The high energy and the static buzz start again, the iris tries to focus, the room seems to get extremely bright, then goes back to normal.]

We each started to filter out the back door into the driveway. Peter placed his recorder in the dining room and took a couple of pictures of its position. Peter left the house and closed the door. We all walked to the back of the property to explore the freshly-dug foundation of the owners' new home being built. After we looked around the freshly dug hole in the field we all headed over to the barn.

Everyone entered and started conducting EVP sessions and taking photographs.

James stuck with Joan and told her that he had asked for protection because of what he thought was at the cottage and particularly in the barn. At that moment the smell of fresh vomit filled his nostrils.

Joan said she could smell a faint odour in the same spot, and that she could hear Jonathan calling his wife's name over and over again: "Angela, Angela."

James noticed the smell was coming back again.

Joan said that, according to Nathan, the smell of vomit was from his wife, Angela. She was taken to the basement to be taught a lesson. She had become scared and vomited.

Once again James chastised Nathan for his treatment of people, and women in particular.

James asked why he had not crossed over. The response through Joan was that there was nothing over there for him. James told him he was wrong and that if he crossed over he would be met by loved ones and no longer be alone.

Joan said he did not understand. James asked if he enjoyed being alone in the basement and having everyone wanting to stay away from him. James explained to him that he had to stop wallowing in self pity and to move on so everyone else trapped there by him could move on as well.

Joan said his response was, "Now you are talking." Joan then said he had left the basement.

Just prior, there was a sound like footsteps on the stairs leaving the basement.

[Back in the cottage, Peter's digital recorder captures an exhale sound, that of a female or young male, followed immediately by a short whine inside the dining room.]

We all returned to the cottage and I invited everyone to view some photos taken of the barn loft during our last investigation.

Joan picked up on someone named John.

James called out, "Is that you, Jonathan? Did you say that you'd give us a thrashing?"

This was immediately followed by a young male's voice moaning, "No!" James reacted to Joan shaking her head and also said, "No?"

"No, that one is … that one is not … he's more younger. I don't know why he died young. He got sick or something; I don't know," Joan explained.

This verified what the visiting medium, Carol, had mentioned regarding John dying from an abrupt fall from a horse at a young age.

The team fanned out and started taking photos room by room, while several of us headed outside to take advantage of the sunlight in getting exterior shots of the cottage.

Joan returned to the main floor studio and commented on a particular painting. The subject's eyes seemed to follow her. A male voice whispered, "What was that?"

Shortly afterward, there is a loud snap, to which Joan asked, "What happened?" A female voice whispered, "You know," very quickly.

Peter placed the digital recorder on the arm of the sofa in the studio and moved to retrieve his camera. Joan sat on the fourth stair leading to the second floor.

Peter hummed a short musical theme, and a male voice whispered, "Fuck." Joan exclaimed, "Oh God, this is cold!" but didn't elaborate.

Peter returned to the studio and activated his camera. Spotting Joan sitting quietly on the stairs, he asked, "Contemplating?" and began taking photos.

Joan began breathing heavier, as she began to cry.

Peter asked Joan, "What are you feeling?" She did not reply, but continued to sob in sad breaths for another thirty seconds. Between sobs, Joan breathed, "God, stop it!"

"What are you feeling?" Peter asked.

"Oh God" — she exhaled — "I couldn't breathe!"

Michelle moved in beside her.

"Do you need a tissue?"

I entered the cottage with James and said, "Hello!"

[The digital recorder captures the voice of an older male saying, "Who's he?"]

"No, I'm okay," Joan replied.

Peter moved toward the washroom, and said, "We're having a situation."

"Who?" I asked, and James and I headed into the studio.

Peter brought a box of tissues to Joan.

"Did you sense somebody doing this to you?"

"Yeah. I felt so cold and I felt like … it's just shivering suddenly and … just choking me. I knew this would happen tonight; I knew it."

"Was this after you sat on the stairs?" Peter asked.

"Yeah."

"You get a sense of who — or male or female — was doing this?"

"That was a male."

"You have a male doing that to you?" James said.

"Yeah."

James was riled up when he spoke next. "Is this what you referred to by giving someone a thrashing — attacking a woman? If you're someone that's here of Scottish descent, you know that that's wrong. Am I right?"

Pause.

James started provoking, "Maybe you're too much of a wimp to take on a man; you'd rather attack a woman! I'm of Scottish descent; I'm not afraid of you!"

"Did you feel hands on you or was it more of an internal?" Peter asked.

"It was inside. I hear, like, uh … he told me once before, 'Don't come, don't come.' Now he said, 'I told you don't come!'"

"And then what happened?" Peter asked.

"And then I felt like, yeah, I couldn't breathe. I had no oxygen."

It sounded like you were getting upset, not in a panic. That's what it looked like. I thought you were being overwhelmed by an emotion."

"You know when someone's grabbing you and you don't know what's going on? It's like your body wants to react, but you can't? That was strange. It's not here, now. I feel cold, but …"

"You think he went upstairs, or is it hard to tell?"

"No, he came from upstairs."

James to Peter, nodding toward the stairs. "Shall we?"

"We shall."

[Upstairs the surveillance microphone records two men.

First male: "What did you do?"

Second male: Unintelligible comment.

First male: "Now look what you did."

Both males start laughing.]

Peter, James, and Joan ascended the stairs to the second floor. Peter suggested "squeezing" the second floor and stayed behind at the top of the staircase as James and Joan wandered into the master bedroom. Peter activated his camera. "Where's the fellow who just did this? Make yourself known, please. You've nowhere to go."

"What's your issue with having Joan here?" James asked.

"Are you afraid she'll find out about you?" Peter asked.

"Yeah, it feels like, no, don't do that," Joan told them.

"What did he do?" James asked Joan.

"He choked someone like that. He was doing it and …"

"Is this the guy with the initials R.T.I.?" Peter asked.

"Does that mean Really Tough Idiot?"

"Or Really Tiny Idiot. You're not so tough. You pick on women? Come up behind them?"

Michelle and I came up the stairs and passed Peter.

[The surveillance camera on the main floor is saturated with extremely high energy, even though our EMF baselines show nothing, all recordings on this camera are fried.]

"He doesn't like women," Joan reported.

"What did a woman ever do to you to make you do that to a woman? Did you get your feelings hurt? Get over it! We all do. Be a man about things. Don't touch women," James yelled out.

"You got a name?" Peter asked.

"Make me vomit," Joan stated.

"Is this John?" Peter asked.

"What did you just say, Joan?" James asked.

"He said, 'They make me vomit.'"

"Women make you vomit?!"

"Well, you wouldn't be here without a woman! What's your name?"

"Jonathan."

"John from the barn? Or a different John?"

"Peter, I was starting to feel it getting colder. I was going to get you to snap a picture this way, so next time you see me pointing at you …" James said.

"Okay, you want me to shoot you? It's getting dark in there, so I don't know if I can see you. What's your last name, John?"

"Yeah, we smelled vomit earlier. Was that you?" I asked.

"Are you still up here with us, John?" Peter asked

"He says, 'Call me Nathan.'" Joan stated.

"Nathan?" Peter said.

"Yes," Joan confirmed.

"Okay, so it's Jonathan, but you prefer to be called Nathan, is that correct?"

"What year is it, Nathan?"

"Eighteen … eighteen … seventy … seventy-two."

"That's funny, Nathan, that you claim to dislike women, but you're communicating through a woman right now. Don't you find that to be a bit of a contradiction? So that was you that said you were going to give us a thrashing? Or was that somebody else that's a little tougher to take on a man? That's very low of you to attack a woman." James pushed for a response.

"You'd better watch it!" Peter said.

"You feel ashamed for acting like that? You should!" James said.

Joan reacted, giggling.

"What did he say?" James asked.

"He said, 'Shut up!'" Joan said, laughing.

"He told me to shut up?!" James asked.

"Well, let's hear from you, Nathan," Peter said.

"Did Joan give you a year?" Peter asked.

"1872."

"Nathan, did you go to church here?" Peter asked.

"What church?"

"This church."

"No."

"There's no church here?"

"No, he doesn't go to church."

"Why don't you go to church?" James asked.

"Women go."

"Oh, I see, so you forgo praising God, just because women are there. What does God think of that?" James called out.

"How old is Nathan?"

"I don't understand why he died young. He died young," Joan said.

"How old were you, Nathan?"

"Thirty ... thirty something. Thirty-four?"

"Do you live here in the house?" Peter asked.

"Yes."

"Do you remember seeing us visit here before?"

There was no reply.

"Were you ever married, Nathan?"

"Why didn't you go into the light Nathan, when you died?" Peter asked.

"I'm not ... I'm not dead," Joan relayed.

"Oh, you're dead," James told him.

"Can you show us what you can do Nathan, if you're not dead? Can you move something? Make a noise that we can all hear?" Peter asked.

"Where are you from, Nathan? Were you born in Canada?" James inquired.

"Yeah. He's trying to ... get in," Joan reported.

"Get in where?" James asked.

"Inside me."

"Tell him to piss off," I told her.

"I felt like he's trying to use my body to do something and I started to just not to let him do this, but he wants ..."

"No, Nathan, leave her alone," Peter commanded.

"If what Joan just said is true, we now have proof that you are a liar, 'cause you told us that you're not dead. If you're not dead, why do you need to try to enter Joan's body or anybody else's body and do something? Are you lying to us? Is your name even Nathan? Did that confuse you? You don't like somebody challenging you?" James said.

"Nathan, what's your surname?" Peter asked.

"He used bad language!" Joan said shyly.

"No, no, I wanna know what he said," James said, angered.

"He said, 'Fuck off!'"

"Okay, you know what Nathan? I had this conversation with you already. You told me to fuck off once before and I told you to fuck off right back. You know what? That's enough of talking like this. We're going to talk like gentlemen, understood? Are you capable of doing that? Or are you a child?"

"No … child …"

"Ahh! So you don't like anybody to call out your maturity or immaturity. You know what Nathan, come out and talk like a man. If you're a man. That's right, 'cause you know I'm right. You're acting like a child."

"You called me a child," Joan said sadly.

"I didn't say you were a child; I said you were acting like a child. There's a big difference," James explained.

"Nathan, did you grow up on this property?" Peter asked.

"Yes."

"Were you born here or did you move here as a child?"

"Was a child here."

"Do you have any brothers or sisters?"

"A brother."

"What did your father do for a living?"

"Farm."

"What was his name?"

"John."

"And that's why you don't want to be called John?" Peter asked.

There was a loud creaking sound mid-way through the loft landing, where no one was present, between Peter and I.

"Did someone just move?" Peter asked.

"No one moved," I told him.

"I just heard a creak here, on the landing," Peter said.

"Something keeps turning my camera off," James reported.

"Is Nathan still with us?" Peter asked.

"Yes."

"It just turned off again. I have a fully charged battery," James stated.

"Nathan, what was your father's surname, please? And don't lie to us," Peter asked.

"Nathan is gone," said Joan.

We all headed back downstairs; James and Joan came down last.

[The surveillance microphone records a male voice: "He's a character."].

Peter suggested bringing out one of the large mirrors from the dining room to do some reflective photography. He carried one out and propped it up in the doorway to the kitchen. Michelle, Joan, and I stepped outside to retrieve Joan's jacket from her car.

Later, on the main floor of the cottage:

In response to Peter asking if anybody was here with the team, Joan referred to the photo of Annie and said, "Definitely this old lady, but I don't know where. I don't know the name. Queen?"

"She's nice though, isn't she?" Peter said.

"Yeah. No, she … I don't know why it came.… They call me 'Queen.'"

"Queen, huh? So you cook and queen?"

James and Joan chuckled.

"John is not her husband, is he?" Peter asked.

"No. They are not related. No, they're not. This one's different."

[There is a long, drawn-out male exhale captured on the digital recorder.]

I advised the team that I would like to try a Spirit Box session upstairs. We all moved back upstairs and I settled on the top step and turned it on.

"Hello?" Peter asked.

Spirit Box — a cheerful voice: "Hello!"

Spirit Box: "We did!"

Peter: "You did what?"

Spirit Box — a male voice, clear but distant: "Wait!"

Spirit Box — a male voice, fuzzier frequency: "Okay."

Peter: "Is somebody with us tonight?"

Spirit Box — a female voice, immediately: "Hi."

Peter: "Hi, hello. How are you?"

Spirit Box: "I'm good."

Spirit Box — a male voice: "I'm good!"

Spirit Box — a male voice: "I'm good!"

Spirit Box: "Funny!"

Spirit Box — a male voice, goofy-sounding, playful: "Hello!"

Spirit Box — a small voice: "Hi."

Peter: "Do you remember us?"

Spirit Box — a male voice: "I did it!"

Peter: "What's my name?"

"We'd like to talk to Harry," I requested.

Spirit Box — a female voice, immediate, indignant-sounding: "Fine!"

Spirit Box — a male voice, fuzzy static: "I don't … believe … you can!"

Spirit Box — a male, disappointed: "Oh, come on!"

Spirit Box: "No problem."

Spirit Box — a male voice: "I hate him."

Spirit Box: "Okay."

Peter: "Henry?"

Spirit Box — a female voice: "Hello?"

Spirit Box: "I hear you."

Spirit Box: "I know!"

Me: "Are you here, Harry?"

There was white noise for twelve seconds.

Me: "Do you know Henry?"

Spirit Box: "Play back."

Spirit Box — a male voice, gruff-sounding: "You will … die!" [A sharp sound, like a gun firing.]

Spirit Box: "Henry!"

Spirit Box — the same gruff-sounding male voice: "Heh heh!"

Me: "Henry? Henry, are you here?"

Spirit Box — a male voice: "Okay."

Spirit Box — a male voice: "I love you."

Spirit Box — a male voice: "I did."

Spirit Box — a male voice, stern and clear: "Bring him up."

Spirit Box — the same gruff-sounding male voice: "I love you."

Spirit Box — a male voice: "I don't."

Peter: "Henry?"

Spirit Box — a male voice, exasperated, voice trailing off: "… believe this …"

Spirit Box — a male voice: "What happened?"

Spirit Box — the same gruff-sounding male voice: "Believe … me."

Spirit Box — a young male or female voice, distant: "Believe me!"

Spirit Box — the same gruff-sounding male voice: "I know."

Spirit Box — a male voice: "I know."

Me: "Amy?"

Spirit Box — a male voice, immediately: "Uh-oh."

Spirit Box — a male voice: "I've got her."

Spirit Box: "Okay."

Me: "Amy?"

Spirit Box — a female voice, immediately: "Hello!" Followed by the clatter of something solid crashing into pieces.

Spirit Box — a female voice: "Hello!"

Spirit Box — a female voice: "Please stop!"

Spirit Box: "What happened?"

Me: "Emma?"

[A female voice is also recorded on the surveillance microphone saying, "Yes." And then a male voice yelling, "Get out."]

Spirit Box — the same gruff-sounding male voice barks: "Go 'way!"

Spirit Box — a female voice, despondent-sounding: "Carl's win."

Spirit Box — the same gruff-sounding male, quickly: " Behind you! Fernando!"

Me: "Is Emma here?

There was white noise for seven seconds.

Me: "Can you talk to us, Emma?"

Spirit Box — a male voice: "Hurt."

Peter, misunderstanding: "Sure?"

Spirit Box — a young male voice: "Want Em?"

Me: "Are there many here?"

Spirit Box — a female voice: "They … want … me."

Spirit Box — the same gruff-sounding male voice: "Eleven."

Spirit Box — a young male voice: "Eleven."

Spirit Box: "Seven."

Peter: "Seven?"

Spirit Box: "Yeah!"

Spirit Box — a male voice: "We should go."

Spirit Box — a male voice: "Okay."

"You were talking earlier to Nathan. Was he lying about his name? Was his name Harry?" I asked.

Spirit Box: Sound of a heavy wooden chair or table scraping/shifting

Spirit Box: "He did!" More wooden scraping sounds as if more than one person is getting up from sitting around a table.

Me: "Carol?"

Spirit Box — a female voice, immediately: "Uh huh?"

Spirit Box — a male voice: "Okay."

Me: "Is Carol here?"

There was white noise for nine seconds.

Spirit Box — a female voice: "Quite."

Me: "Emma, can you tell us what year it is, please?"

As soon as "Emma" was mentioned, sound bursts began again.

Spirit Box — a male voice, quickly: "No! Don't tell him!"

Spirit Box: "What?"

Spirit Box — a deep male voice: "I won't."

Spirit Box — a male voice: "Okay. Okay."

Spirit Box — a male voice: "What?"

Spirit Box — a male voice, quickly: "Who's that?!"

Spirit Box: "Okay."

Spirit Box — a higher-pitched voice: "Okay!"

Spirit Box — a male voice: "Okay! Okay!"

Spirit Box — a male voice: "Okay."

Spirit Box — a male voice: "Okay!"

Me: "What year is it, Emma?"

There was white noise for eight seconds.

Me: "Do you live in this house?"

There was white noise for several seconds.

Spirit Box: "You!"

Spirit Box — a male voice: "Time ..."

Spirit Box: "Time!"

Spirit Box — a male voice: "Prick!"

Spirit Box: "I know!"

Spirit Box — a male voice: "Uh huh!"

Spirit Box — a female voice: "Hey Dick! Watch the lip!"

Spirit Box — a male voice: "Who, me?"

Spirit Box — the same female voice: "Go on!"

Me: "What year did you move into this house?"

Spirit Box — a high-pitched female voice gasps, as if suddenly spooked.

Spirit Box — a male voice: "Mommy?"

Me: "Can you tell me again, Emma, what year did you move in to this house?"

Again, at the very mention of the name, "Emma," radio bursts started to erupt under my voice, as if protesting.

Spirit Box — a female voice: "Oh no. He knows ... my name!"

Spirit Box — a male voice: "Shut ... your lip!"

Spirit Box — a male sneezes.

Joan: "Amy."

Spirit Box: "Bless you."

Me: "Hmm?"

Joan: "Amy."

Me: "Yeah, there's an Amy here as well."

Spirit Box: "Uh huh!"

Joan, referring to Annie's photo: "This is that lady? What's that one's name?"

Spirit Box — a male voice, quickly: "Help you out."

Spirit Box — a male voice: "Thank you."

Peter: "Did you just say, 'Thank you'"?

Joan: "I feel like she would call herself, 'Queen,' or something."

Spirit Box — a female voice: "Oh dear!"

Me: "Who?"

Peter: "The old woman in the picture?"

Joan: "Old woman, yeah."

Spirit Box: "Oh boy!"

Spirit Box — a male voice: "What now?"

Joan: "She's like, uh ... medicine ... it's like a doctor, or nurse, or something."

Me: "Midwife?"

Joan: "Yes. Something like that, yeah."

Richard: "Amy?"

Spirit Box — a female voice, immediately: "Uh huh?"

Me: "Amy, are you a midwife?"

Me: "Emma?"

Spirit Box — a high-pitched female voice, panicked: "Please ... tell him ... I go!"

Spirit Box: "I will."

Me: "Is Amy here?"

Spirit Box: "Amy."

Spirit Box — a female voice: "I'm in!"

Spirit Box: "Forget you!"

Me: "Who is Miriam? Who is Miriam to you?"

There are four seconds of silence.

Spirit Box — a female voice, quickly: "My hope."

Spirit Box — a female voice: "We'll leave … that other … for Dick."

Spirit Box: "Quiet. That's right."

Spirit Box — a male voice: "Yes.

Me: "Is Miriam downstairs?"

Spirit Box: "You hear that?"

Spirit Box — a high-pitched female voice: "I love … [Indistinguishable]"

Spirit Box — a female voice: " Spiritual."

Spirit Box: "Thank you."

Peter: "Is somebody in the cellar of the barn, looking after it?"

Spirit Box, quickly: "Don't know."

Spirit Box — a female voice, quickly: "It's him."

Spirit Box — a female voice, loud and clear: "Greetings."

Spirit Box: "Shut up."

Peter: "Me?"

Spirit Box, erupting in another flurry of replies: "Me."

Spirit Box — a male voice: "No, me."

Spirit Box — a female voice: "Whatever."

Spirit Box — a female voice: "Whatever."

Spirit Box: "So there!"

Spirit Box — a male voice: "Release it."

Spirit Box — a male voice, clear: "Grab it!"

Spirit Box — a male voice: "Grab it."

Spirit Box — a male voice: "Got it."

Spirit Box — a male voice: "Okay … we're done."

Spirit Box — a young male or female voice: "The leg's gone."

From the Spirit Box came a pair of loud reports, possibly a gunshot, followed by something solid falling loudly.

Peter: "Is there somebody there protecting something?"

There was white noise for five seconds.

Peter: "Yes or no?"

White noise for another five seconds.

Peter: "Are they there right now?"

Spirit Box — a male voice: "Careful."

Spirit Box — a deep male voice: "Hurry."

Spirit Box: "For what?"

Spirit Box — a male voice: "Where is he?"

Spirit Box: "Down there."

Spirit Box: Cat meow.

Spirit Box: "High-pitched kitty!"

Peter: "Will they mind if we dig in the cellar?"

Spirit Box, immediately: "Uh-huh!"

Spirit Box — a male voice: "Go 'way!"

White noise: Eleven seconds

Peter: "Are you angry that the field has been torn up by tractors?"

Spirit Box — a male voice, quietly: "Are we …"

Spirit Box — a male voice: "Don't know yet."

Spirit Box — a low, deep male voice: "We're not."

Spirit Box — a male voice, loudly: "Go 'way! Go home!"

Spirit Box — a male voice chimed in: "Go away."

Spirit Box — a male voice, quickly: "Go away!"

Spirit Box — a male voice: "Go away. Get outta here!"

Spirit Box — a male voice: "Go 'way! Go home!"

Spirit Box — a male voice, clear: "Mahatz!"

Spirit Box — a male voice: "What do you mean?"

Spirit Box — a female voice: "Came through!"

Spirit Box — a gruff male voice, barking: "Again! Hello?"

I shut down the Spirit Box.

Peter asked, "Is there anybody here who would like to hear some music? We brought music, again." Pause. "Would you like to hear some music? Joan, are you hearing anything?"

"No."

Soon after, everyone descended the staircase for the studio.

[A male voice is captured on the camera microphone saying, "Get back."]

"Is there anybody down here who would like to hear music? Is it okay if we go out to the barn?" Peter asked.

"Yeah, let's go out to the barn," I said.

"Finally, somebody answered, great!"

Peter, Michelle, and I left the cottage and closed the door, joining James and Joan, already outside. Eventually, the group made its way to the barn. Peter walked around it on the east/road-side and reported feeling tense in his stomach as he approached. He met Richard and Michelle at the door. James and Joan were the last to arrive.

Just inside the barn, as the team stood quietly, there was a low growl. Preceding the growl, there was an extremely light, male whisper saying "They're going after me."

Then immediately after, almost just as slight, a second male voice said, "Help him, boy."

I heard several noises coming from the loft, and Joan wandered into the cellar without a word, a flashlight, or turning on the light.

Peter closed the door to the barn, in case any stray coyotes felt the need to investigate the barn with the team inside it.

Peter entered the storage area and asked several questions, and I joined him there. James and Michelle joined Joan downstairs.

Peter reported feeling like a small cobweb was tickling his right eyebrow.

"Do the flashes bother you?" Peter asked.

[His digital recorder captures an older male's voice replying, "Yes," in a matter-of-fact tone.]

I moved the photo of barn boy away from the landing to the ladder for the loft so I could climb up alone. Peter walked deeper into the metal shop and felt tension in his stomach, as if anxious to be in the barn at that moment.

Joan, James, and Michelle emerged from the cellar.

"We are close to something," Joan said.

"In what way? Close to finding something, or ..." Peter inquired.

"Yes, because that older male spirit was downstairs; just a few seconds ago, he got so worried, he just went upstairs. Come here. Maybe it's here — the thing you are looking for."

Michelle started making her way up into the loft. James climbed next, followed by Joan. Peter set the E. Probe 1.0 on the air conditioning unit and armed it then descended into the darkened cellar alone and sat on the upturned cinder block farthest away from the stairs.

Peter asked several questions in the dark, taking photos and trying to provoke responses respectfully. He examined some of his photos and, spying nothing out of the ordinary, said, "I'm not very good at that. You know who is good at that? Paul! Do you remember Paul?"

The E. Probe alarmed a couple of seconds after Peter's question about Paul and stayed alarmed until Peter left the cellar and turned it off.

In the loft James was having trouble with his camera being able to focus. We were doing a sweep with the parabolic microphone.

Joan was concentrating but not receiving any information.

Peter reset the E. Probe and left it by the door to the barn, again, noting one must touch it directly to set it off. He moved into the storage area, putting his back to the garage door, and turned his flashlight off. For a split second he thought he had seen somebody walk west. It was like a white form.

There was a loud wooden thump. Peter inquired, but no one had opened and closed the loft door. I told him that Joan had heard the noise as well.

[On the parabolic microphone comes a woman's scream, but it is impossible to determine if this was paranormal or someone outside.]

Peter descended into the cellar again, keeping the light off. He turned his Spirit Box on, hoping to use it to hear responses. He heard a male voice that said, "Creep!"

Peter began the Spirit Box session as the rest of the team descended and gathered around on the ground floor.

Peter: "Hello?"

Spirit Box: White noise

Peter: "Who's here with me?"

Spirit Box: White noise.

Peter: "Will you tell me your name, please?"

Spirit Box — a male voice: "Come no more."

Peter: "Hey, I just want to talk."

Spirit Box — a male voice: "Shut it."

Peter: "Yeah, with you. Come on, man! I'm here in the dark! Are you afraid of me?"

Spirit Box: White noise for a long time.

Peter: "What's going to happen if we dig here, tonight?

Spirit Box: White noise.

Peter: Speak up, please. What are you going to do if we start digging tonight?"

Spirit Box — a male voice: "Help us."

Peter: "Are you gonna thrash us?"

Spirit Box — a female voice: "A boy!"

Peter: "Is there a young boy here?"

Spirit Box: The white noise drops an octave.

Spirit Box — a male voice: "Just dig him!"

Peter: "Please don't be afraid. What's your name?"

Peter: "Pardon? What's your name?"

Spirit Box: White noise for a long time; it drops an octave again, but nothing discernible is heard.

Peter: "Is your name Jackie?

Spirit Box: White noise.

Peter: "Is your name Mark? Mark? I think I heard you. Is that you, Mark?"

Spirit Box: White noise.

Spirit Box — a male voice: "Dig ... for Mark."

Spirit Box — a male voice, agreeing: "Uh huh."

Peter: "What's the name of the tall guy who works here?"

Spirit Box: White noise.

Peter: "Someone told me there was a tall guy who works down here."

Spirit Box — a male voice: "Get ... out."

Peter: "Was that you, just now? I thought I heard a comment there."

Spirit Box — a female voice: "Leave."

Peter: "Leave? Why?"

Spirit Box — a male voice, even more distant, shouting: "Don't go!"

Peter: "I'm just visiting."

Spirit Box: A metallic-sounding impact.

Peter: "Did you hurt anybody in your lifetime?"

Spirit Box — a male voice: "You bet ... I did!"

After some more speechless white noise, Peter switched the direction to FM forward. Michelle, who had come down into the cellar in the dark during the session to take photos, shared some news: "You know when it said, 'Leave'? And then you said, 'Why should I leave?' behind you, it said you were trouble."

"Oh, okay! 'Trouble', eh? What kind of trouble? Will I be in trouble? Will I be in trouble if I start digging down here, tonight?"

Spirit Box — a female voice: "We're too ..."

Peter: "Pardon?"

Spirit Box — a female voice: "Go ... down the stair."

Peter: "You know, if I'm going to be in so much trouble, I'd appreciate knowing who's going to be the source of my punishment."

Spirit Box — a faint female voice: "Doesn't help ..."

Peter: "If I cause trouble, what's the name of the person that's going to do something about it?

Spirit Box: White noise.

Peter: "Or don't you have a name?"

Spirit Box: White noise.

Peter: "C'mon, what are you afraid of? I'm standing here in the dark; you could come at me from any side!

Spirit Box: White noise.

Peter: "I can't see you!

Spirit Box: White noise.

Peter: "What the hell?!"

Spirit Box — a female voice, urging: "Go!"

Peter tried to wait in silence for a short time before asking more questions. "Now are you happy that the sound is off?" No response. "Man, it's quiet, down here! I can't believe it!" Peter asked several more questions and received no responses. Joan stepped down into the cellar, commenting on the coldness, and James followed her.

"Is it all right if we dig now?" Peter asked.

Joan, amused: "Hmph!"

Peter: "What?"

Joan: "You're not going to find anything."

Peter: "Oh, really? Was Joan right? Is there a box down here, somewhere?"

Joan: "He says like this. 'Not answering!'"

Peter, scoffing: "You're funny. So we're just going to find it on our own, right? Why is it such a big deal to you? You're dead!"

Joan: "He's laughing."

Peter: "Well, that's fine."

Joan: "Can you hear it?"

Peter: "I can't hear it. You can have a good laugh all you want but, the fact of the matter is, you don't have a physical form anymore. Your body has passed on. So my question to you is, why does it matter if we find or don't find what's buried down here? Why do you care?"

Joan: "You will know me."

Peter: "Well, we're getting to know you, anyway. We're not the police. What are you afraid of?"

Joan: "Not answering."

Peter: "So you're going to clam up like a kid? A child?"

Joan, immediately: "Ouch! Shit!"

Me: "What happened?"

James: "What's the matter?"

Joan: "It uh … pinched me!"

Peter: "In your left thigh? Back of your left thigh?"

Joan: "Yeah."

Peter, calmly: "Don't do that. I'm the one talkin' to ya!"

James: "He won't pinch a man; he'll pinch a woman. Right, Nathan? 'Cause you don't like women?"

Joan: "It's so funny tonight! He's attacking me, [he] says, 'It's your fault, your doing … Why you came …'"

Peter: "Mmm. Because you're the one who can tell us probably, right?"

James: "So he's being playful with you?"

Peter: "Yeah, in a nasty kind of way."

Joan: "He doesn't hate me, but he knows I will tell you most of the thing; not everything."

Peter: "Right, because you're the …"

Joan: "I didn't tell you everything, yet. But yeah, this one was … nice one."

Peter, scoffing: "If that was nice! Are you the one who choked her?"

Joan: "It's like … pinched, or something went to my … I can feel it, still."

Peter: "C'mon, leave her alone."

James: "Peter wants you to pinch him."

Peter: "Sure!"

Joan, soberly: "Won't answer."

Peter: "So you won't answer, that's fine. We'll continue to dig; we have permission. So the only reason I can think of that you don't want to be known is because you have something to hide. A crime, perhaps? Did you kill somebody?"

Joan: "He says, 'Why are you asking me that?'"

Peter: "Because we're curious. We've been told that there's a body down here; somebody was buried here — maybe even more than one person!"

Joan: "His Grandma …"

Peter: "Pfft! Your Gran-what?! I chuckle at the thought."

Joan, serious: "His Grandma."

James: "Why did you bury your Grandmother down here?"

Peter: "Are you a member of the Menzies family?"

Joan: "It's so funny … the character he has. It's like he just said 'Tch!' like that."

Peter: "Like I got it wrong? I'm reaching?"

Joan: "Yeah."

Peter: "So, was your Grandma named Isabella?"

Joan, after a pause, slowly: "No …"

Peter: "No? Okay, well I have to ask, because she's missing, that's all. We don't know where she's buried. Do you know who I'm talking about?"

Joan: "No."

Peter: "Okay. I'm talking about somebody who was before your time, I guess" — he paused — "I don't even know who I'm talking to. Is this Jonathan?" — another pause — "Nathan?"

Joan: "It's both."

Peter: "Both. You're both down here?"

Joan: "No, it's both, it's …"

James: "Jonathan and Nathan are the same person, right?"

Peter: "Oh, I thought Jonathan was the dad …"

James: "He prefers 'Nathan.'"

Joan: "No, his dad is John and his name is Jonathan and they call him Nathan."

Peter: "The son."

Joan: "Yes."

Peter: "Okay."

Me: "I'm going to go up and check that, uh … it sounds like they're pretty frickin' close." A short discussion ensues about the proximity of the howling coyote pack outside the barn.

Peter: "Hey Nathan, are you sending the coyotes our way?"

Joan: "No."

Peter: "Oh, you sent them here. You've got that power, have you? So you've got the power over animals, but you don't have the power to talk."

Joan, soberly: "Just leave me alone."

Peter: "Oh, we will, but we just need some answers, like your last name.

[*The digital recorder captures a male voice, half-whispered, sounding like, "Barry" or "Barret."*]

Joan: "Starts with … 'B.' 'Bur—'"

Peter, immediately: "Augh, I'm getting a pain right here at the top of my head, just now as you were saying that. I felt like right here, there was a poke at my head. I'm sorry, I didn't catch that last name. Are you really tall, Nathan? Are you the tall man that people have said works down here?"

Suddenly, I called out to signal the arrival of the owners' lost pet cat. The team headed back upstairs to try and retrieve it safely. Eventually Joan picked the cat up and said, "I know he sent you here — to distract us! We ask him so many questions."

The team headed back to the cottage with the cat.

[The digital recorder captures a definite gun or rifle shot.]

I contacted the owners and let them know that we had their cat, and the investigation was on standby until they arrived to the collect the pet.

The team moved upstairs in the second floor of the cottage. Peter set his E. Probe on the kitchen counter and left the digital recorder in the staircase alcove before he walked upstairs with his pendulum. Peter conducted a pendulum session that wasn't very successful.

Peter asked Joan if she picked up on anything from the master bedroom. She claimed there was a woman present who was not communicating, but listening. Peter offered to play some music.

Peter descended the stairs to retrieve the CD player; he picked up the recorder as he climbed back up. "Rock of Ages," choir version, began.

Michelle relayed Joan's message from the woman that she didn't like this music because "she's not old."

Peter skipped to "Silver Threads Among the Gold" (1873). Peter asked Joan if this song was "too old," too. It was. He turned it off.

I asked Joan to ask the woman which year she prefered. Joan didn't respond directly but said the woman's husband didn't like the music she liked. "That's why she's not allowed to listen to music."

Joan asked, "Do you have baby music?" Peter offered children's music instead. As he set up the vintage children's music CD, Joan continued to relay what she'd picked up from the "woman."

Joan: "She lost a baby. It was a boy."

James: "Is that who's buried in the barn?"

Joan: "No, that's another person."

James: "Is the son buried in the barn?"

Joan: "It was an accident."

James: "Nathan accidentally killed him, maybe?"

"The Laughing Policeman" (1926) started playing.

[Immediately an older female voice is recorded on the surveillance micro-phone saying, "Oh gracious."]

While the singer (Charles Penrose) laughed during the first chorus, Joan reported on behalf of the woman that this song, "makes her nervous." Peter and I laughed at the suggestion.

"How can a laughing guy make you nervous? Come on!" Peter said.

"He's laughing like her husband," Michelle said, relaying information from Joan.

Michelle stated, "She doesn't like this at all." Peter moved to change the CD track to "The Prune Song."

James: "Got any Beatles? Everybody likes The Beatles."

Peter: "I didn't come here to deejay!"

"The Wedding of the Painted Doll" began as I attempted a pendulum session along with Peter.

Me: "Is there an Emma here?"

Peter: "I've got a 'yes.' How about you?"

Me: "I've got a ... neutral."

Peter: "Oh, it [the circling pendulum] is growing. [Pause] Is there an Amy here?"

Me: "I'm getting 'yes.'"

Peter: "And mine's growing. Wow! Amy?"

Me: "Do you know Harry? [Pause] Getting, 'yes.'"

Peter: "Yeah, me too. 'Yes.'"

Me: "Is Harry a good person?"

Peter: "Yes." The swing of the pendulum growing stronger.

Me: "Are you related to Harry?"

Peter: "Still 'yes'; slowing down, actually."

Me: "Hm-mm, me too."

Peter: "I've almost stopped. You still here, Amy? [Pause] 'Neutral.' Emma, are you here?"

Me: "Going 'neutral.'"

Peter: "I'm still 'neutral.' Harry, are you here? ["The Wedding of the Painted Doll" ends.] Still 'neutral.' Slowing down even more, like ..." ["Barnacle Bill the Sailor" begins.]

Me: "Henry, are you here? Is that you, Henry?"

Peter: "Starting to go 'yes,' slowly. Henry, is this you? [Pause] Oh, this is really large 'yes' now. Henry?"

Me: "Henry, are you in charge of this house?"

Peter: "Slowing down. On mine, anyway."

Me: "Henry, are you in charge of this house?"

Peter: "'Neutral' for me."

Me: "I'm getting a 'yes.' [Pause] Do you take your orders from somebody else? Henry? [Pause] Big 'yes.'"

Peter: "Mine's 'neutral.'"

Me: "Do you know Miriam?" [Pause] "Do you know Miriam?"

Peter: "Mine's slowing almost right down to a full stop."

Me: "I get a 'yes.'"

Peter: "Maybe that's because you're asking the questions."

Me: "Could be."

Peter: "I'm completely stopped. Is there anybody else besides you, Harry, and the five of us?" [Pause] "Shaking."

Me: "Do you know Nathan?"

Peter: "Mine's absolutely still. Do you know Nathan? Small 'yes'; growing a little bit, but shaking."

Me: "Is Nathan here?" [Pause] "Is Nathan here?"

Peter: "Just shaking."

Me: "I get a 'no.'"

Peter: "Starting to go small 'yes' but shaking."

Me, in a disbelieving tone: "Nathan, are you here?"

Peter: "Yes."

Me: "Do you like this music?"

Peter: "Growing 'yes,' on here." [Pause] "Getting larger; 'yes.' Almost in time with the music." [the song concludes.] "Should we stop the music, Nathan?" ["The Runaway Train" begins.] "Slowing down." [Pause] "I'll ask again. Should we stop the music?" [Pause] "Small 'no.'"

Me: "Is it okay if we stop the music?"

Peter: "'No' is growing."

Me: "You're getting 'no'?"

Peter: "Yeah. [It's] growing. Yep, 'no.' So it's all right if we keep playing it?" [Pause] "Slowing down."

Me: "Can we play more music for you?"

Peter: "'Yes.' It just changed direction, here. Getting larger. Thank you, Getting larger. Thank you." [Pause] "Does this music make you feel happy?" [Pause] "Big 'yes.'" [Pause] "Does it remind you of happier times?" [Pause] "'Big 'yes.'" [Long pause] "Now that you're in a good mood, would it be a good time for us to dig in the barn?" [Pause] "'Yes'? Would you show us where to dig in the barn, if we brought the music with us?" [Pause] "'Yes'? So no harm would come to us if you came with us and the music came along?" [Pause] "Slowing down ... neutral. You're not sure." [Pause] "If we went to the barn and we brought the music and it made you happy, would you show us where to dig, please?" [Pause] "Swinging neutrally." [Pause; the song ended.] "You're not sure?" ["The Teddy Bears' Picnic" began.] "Would you like us to carry on playing the music here in the cottage instead?" [Pause] "Growing 'yes.' Very pronounced 'yes.' You really are afraid of the barn, or you don't want anyone in the barn, is that right?" [Long pause as Michelle settles.] "Nathan, is this still you?" [Pause] "Do you know Isabella?"

[There is an odd, breath-like exhale on the digital recorder.]

Peter's Pendulum: slowing down.

Peter: "Do you know Isabella?"

Peter's pendulum: neutral.

Peter: "Yes or no? Do you know who I'm talking about?"

Peter's pendulum: neutral. Slowing right down to a stop, almost.

I stood up and headed downstairs.

Peter: "You're being very stubborn, aren't you? There are certain questions you don't like."

James: "I'm picturing an old cartoon with skeletons and stuff with that music."

Peter: "I'm going to stop this session right now because my arm's getting tired."

James and I left the cottage for the barn to retrieve the large Barn Boy photo as "Who's Afraid of the Big Bad Wolf?" started.

Michelle took photos of the smaller bedroom and tried to explain the light phenomenon she picked up from inside the closet. Peter suggested it was likely bouncing light from a nearby picture frame.

"Grandfather's Clock" started as Michelle observed that another photo she had taken showed a similar light pattern in open space inside the closet and agreed it must have been caused by a reflection. Peter got up and went downstairs with the recorder for a sip of coffee.

[Beginning with a female-sounding exhale, the tonal quality of the air steadily grows louder and a female voice is heard whispering, "Handled it like a lady!"]

Peter moved to place his flashlight on the counter with a loud bang. The recorder was completely static, lying on the kitchen counter, hence debunking the idea the recorder itself was being moved through the air, causing the audible environmental change.

"Popeye the Sailorman" began upstairs. Peter started back up with his coffee.

Michelle reported feeling a cold area at the top of the stairs. Peter carried on into the bedroom and sat on the bed and set up in there.

"Ragtime Cowboy Joe" began; the whole team was together on the second floor again. Peter attempted pendulum communication but received no results. Joan claimed she saw some light phenomenon pass in front of James.

I began another pendulum session. Peter decided to try again, as well.

Me: "Can you identify this boy? [Indicating the Barn Boy photo] Can you identify this boy in this photograph?"

Peter: "Mine started rocking side-to-side, now it's changing; sort of stopped. It went up and down, a little bit. It can't decide."

Me: You don't know who this boy is?

Pendulum: large no.

Me: "This photograph was taken in the barn. Is there any reason why this boy would be in the barn?

Pendulum: neutral.

Me: "You don't know?"

Peter: "Neutral."

Me: "Yup."

Peter: "Well, that was a big help."

Michelle: "Ask if it's Mark."

Richard: "Is this boy's name Mark?"

Pendulum: no.

Richard: "Is this boy's name Ricky? Is his name Ricky?"

Pendulum: yes.

Peter: "This one's starting to swing, too. Is that boy's name Rick, or Ricky?"

Me: "Thank you."

Peter: "Small yes."

Me: "Is his last name Hamilton?" (The last name of the teen killed in the 1960s.)

Peter's pendulum: small yes, but hesitant-like.

Me: "Is his name Hamilton?"

Peter: "It's growing a little bit; 'yes.' What've you got? Not sure?"

I shook my head.

Peter: "I'll ask. Is that boy's name Hamilton?"

Pendulum: growing yes.

Peter: "Does his name sound like Ricky?"

Pendulum: growing yes.

Peter: "Is it, Jackie?"

Pendulum: slowing yes.

Peter: "Hmm. You don't seem so sure. Are you sure? His full name was Jackie Hamilton?"

Pendulum: growing yes.

The surveillance camera microphone recorded Peter asking about Barn Boy.

Peter: "Does the name sound like Ricky?"

[A male voice, "Richard."]

Peter: "Did you get hit by a vehicle?"

[A male voice, "Bicycle."]

Me: "Ask if he died in the train crash."

Peter: "Did Jackie die in the train crash?"

Pendulum: starting to slow down. Neutral.

Peter: "Is that how Jackie died?"

Pendulum: just hanging and slowing down.

Peter: "Did he die here on the property?"

Pendulum: small no, and growing.

Me: "Was he hit by a vehicle while riding his bicycle?"

Peter: "Neutral."

Joan spoke, simultaneously.

Peter: "Is Joan in the other room?"

Joan: "I'm here."

Peter: "Did you just say something?"

Joan: "Yes, I said, 'bicycle.'"

Peter: "So, did Jackie get hit …"

Joan: "It's not Jackie; it's Mark."

Peter: "Sorry?"

Joan: "It's Mark."

Peter: "Was he hit while riding a bicycle? A half-strong 'yes.' Stronger than a small 'yes,' but not a huge whopping circle; but getting stronger now that I'm mentioning it! Thank you. Was Jackie fifteen years old when he died? Slowing down … Are you thinking about it? Was Jackie fifteen? Small 'no' and growing. Was Jackie younger than fifteen? Slowing down and going neutral again. Small 'yes' So he was younger than fifteen. Does he come to visit the barn often in spirit? 'Yes.'"

[The surveillance camera records a bright yellow orb that moves past James in the hall.]

Me: "Does he know someone here?"

Peter: "Does he know somebody here? 'Yes.' Hmm. Did Jackie know a member of the Smith family? 'Yes' growing."

Me: "If the family had kids here, would they have gone to the same school?"

Peter: "I would've thought so."

Me: "I would've thought so as well."

Peter: "But why they wouldn't have class photos from that era, I don't know."

Peter stopped the pendulum.

Peter: "But they had 1945, which seems a little before their time."

We ended the session and as the team started to pack up the equipment Peter and I headed out to the barn to retrieve the pair of shovels. Peter called out to Ricky, then to Jackie. He coughed, feeling a choking sensation before bidding the spirits goodbye and exiting.

Conclusions:

- This investigation continued the overt amount of unfriendly, aggressive, threatening phenomena on the property, which became "physical" toward the team.
- The previous owner reported her kids used to call the cottage's second floor the "spook room."
- Joan was attacked from behind on the staircase in the cottage, corroborated by the second-floor surveillance camera.
- Alleged encounter with "Nathan" (circa 1872) in cottage loft; James stood up to "him" and provoked him heavily.
- Very successful Spirit Box session with many direct responses to the team and sounds of gun reports, furniture being moved loudly and a cat meow.
- Joan reported being pinched in the barn cellar as Peter pushed for answers from a male spirit she was picking up on.
- Peter coughed and reported a choking sensation: a parting warning?

14

FINAL ANALYSIS

Although a great deal of mysteries remained at this location, I felt that a lot of the signs we were seeing indicated something bigger — possibly more sinister — was stationed at this property. We couldn't deny the roving smells of urine and human excrement usually associated with evil. As for the little grey entities that appeared as children through the mediums, somewhat confirmed by the pendulum sessions, I believed it better to err on the side of caution. The biggest indicator of danger was the physical attacks suffered by the team — pains, dizziness, injury and being choked — that told me it was time to end the investigation. Furthermore, these entities, without hesitation, appeared in our private homes — that's when it became personal. When bad-minded spirits do such things there is normally something truly evil behind them, something else unseen that operated like a quarterback behind the scenes, directing and empowering them to carry out such deeds. I had to consider the safety of my team and the members of our families, not to mention the safety of the homeowners, who gave me this report:

> There was an interesting event that happened the day we arrived at the cottage. We were about to move in temporarily as our new home was being built. We entered through the rear door into the hallway and were immediately

assaulted by the odour of feces. Unbelievably horrid, it quickly transformed into the even more disturbing scent of "something dead." Our daughter entered the house but had to leave, holding her hand over her nose and mouth, confirming the smell of death.

On inspection of the hall's attic entrance, as well as going into the crawlspace, we found they were scent free. These locations, by the way, are close to the original chimney location.

My daughter came back into the house asking us to stay at her home and not move in. I was so frustrated, I told the [spirit] residents firmly that this had to stop or I would burn the house to the ground. I assured them of the seriousness of my threat. I repeated these words twice.

The smell slowly dissipated. The next day there was a slight odour but once again I affirmed my words of the day before.

There has not been a recurrence. The building retains its unique "old" building perfume but we are not under attack.

After all the work we did trying to figure out the Barn Boy photos — correspondence with the manufacturer of the camera, trying to recreate the photos, and even questioning a long term resident believing she had recognized the face of a deceased boy from her past — it was an independent analysis of the photos that showed some very peculiar information with regards to the series of pictures from the barn. The metadata from the photos showed the first two barn pictures were taken on September 27 at 20:35:59 and 20:36:10 respectively. The face of Barn Boy and a greenish mist were taken on August 17 at 19:28:52 and 19:29:47 respectively. The last three pictures in the series were all taken on September 27 at 20:36:27, 20:37:27, and 20:37:52.

All photos are in sequence starting at DSC 1515, 1516, 1517, 1518, 1519, 1520 and 1521.

The photos were in perfect sequence and yet the middle two photos show metadata suggesting that they were taken a month prior. This in itself seemed very strange, however following our own protocol only added to the mystery. Paul is old-school and doesn't own a computer system of any kind. He would arrive at my house prior to heading out for an investigation and I would download any data and images he had from previous investigations, clear his card, and start fresh. This was done every time. Several people suggested that old pictures on a camera which have been deleted from the scan disk are not really gone and can, on occasion, make their way back onto the disk. It is plausible that somehow the photos, if they did exist at one time on the scan disk, could reappear after being deleted; however Paul stood firm that they would have never been on his camera prior to this investigation.

All these possible explanations raise so many questions about these photos. Can images just show up from nowhere? I don't know, however I have seen the reverse on several occasions. In 1999 while working on my first book we did some EVP recordings during our investigations. The recordings were made on a mini tape recorder. We had captured a male voice saying he was going to get us. The tape was reviewed by four of us. The next day the tape was blank. It gets stranger — three days later, the recordings were back on the tape.

At the Scarborough Guild investigation we captured an image of an odd, jelly-like orb about the size of a basketball moving past the camera and down the hall landing onto the floor, then wobbling and moving off into an adjacent room. It displayed every color of the rainbow within it. The team reviewed it, and we were completely perplexed because the original colors were brilliant and amazing. The big mystery was that the camera used at the time was black and white. The second mystery was that when we brought in an independent person to look at the images, they no longer existed on the tape. The tape was checked and found to be of the same length and time, nothing was edited, removed, replaced, or blacked-out.

In another investigation we had set up a night vision camera outside looking across a backyard, toward a forest. The night was damp and the camera was picking up moisture in the air moving in waves, which we all saw on the monitor. Over time, the image changed to a scene out of horror movie, with a stone alter and six hooded figures standing around it. When we played the tape back, these images were not there. However, a team member had the good sense to photograph the monitor catching the image.

When dealing with the paranormal it's a given that we will face a great deal of mysteries, some of which are never solved. That is, after all, what it's all about.

It wasn't long after we had shut down this project that I was contacted by the owners. They felt there were too many mysteries remaining and wanted us to continue our investigations. The request would have to be weighed by the team. Should we return in hopes we could answer some of the questions the owners had even if it could come at the cost of our personal safety?

Also by Richard Palmisano

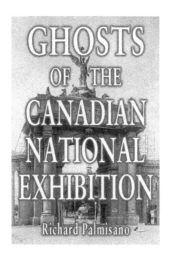

Ghosts of the Canadian National Exhibition

When one thinks of Toronto's Canadian National Exhibition, memories of bright lights, cotton candy, the rush of people, and the excitement of rides spring to mind. But when the lights go down and the people head home, the fairground takes on a life of its own. The spirits that dwell there from the exhibition's long history come out to play and work, even to scare the occasional employee.

The grounds and buildings of the CNE are so richly steeped in history that they are a magnificent storehouse of energy. This area has been in continuous use since before the eighteenth century, starting with Fort Rouille in 1750 and Fort York in 1793. From murders to accidents, it is no surprise that Exhibition Place is haunted. There are many reasons for spirits to dwell in that site, but it may be the joy and excitement that tempts them to linger. These spirits carried the pride and accomplishment of being part of something grand, something that will live on beyond them. That's the true spirit of the Canadian National Exhibition.